ASSESSING AND EVALUATING HONORS PROGRAMS AND HONORS COLLEGES: A PRACTICAL HANDBOOK

Rosalie Otero
University of New Mexico

and

Robert Spurrier
Oklahoma State University

Co-Chairs, NCHC Assessment and Evaluation Committee

Jeffrey A. Portnoy
Georgia Perimeter College
jportnoy@gpc.edu

General Editor, NCHC Monograph Series

Patricia Ann Speelman
Executive Director

National Collegiate Honors Council
1100 Neihardt Residence Center
University of Nebraska–Lincoln
540 N. 16th Street
Lincoln, NE 68588-0627
402-472-9150
Fax: 402-472-9152

http://www.NCHChonors.org

ISBN #0-9773623-1-0

University of Nebraska–Lincoln Printing & Copy Services

ASSESSING AND EVALUATING HONORS PROGRAMS AND HONORS COLLEGES

A PRACTICAL HANDBOOK

Rosalie Otero, University of New Mexico
Robert Spurrier, Oklahoma State University
Co-Chairs, NCHC Assessment and Evaluation Committee

TABLE OF CONTENTS

APPENDICES

PREFACE

Systematic use of evaluation and assessment is one of the core principles guiding education. A considerable portion of current educational research addresses the effectiveness of evaluation and assessment at all levels of education. The relevance of assessment and evaluation has been dramatically increased by the current political tendency to decentralize the responsibility for educational processes. At the same time, students and parents are becoming more aware of differences in quality between schools and programs and more inclined to hold faculty and administrators accountable for their institutions' achievements. Both developments have led to a need for setting explicit standards for educational outcomes.

Assessing and Evaluating Honors Programs and Honors Colleges: A Practical Handbook is intended to serve as an on-campus companion and guide for Honors administrators by helping them to establish new practices or to strengthen established ones. Basically, this monograph provides assistance from both theoretical and practical perspectives by suggesting rationales for assessment and evaluation and offering practical ideas for implementing or strengthening assessment and evaluation practices for Honors Programs and Honors Colleges.

The reader will find rationales and objectives for evaluation and assessment practices as well as specific methods for using Honors consultants and Honors external reviewers. This monograph presents practical approaches to undertaking an Honors self-study, and it includes a self-study outline in the Appendices. Because Honors Programs and Honors Colleges differ widely in terms of administration, structure, curriculum, requirements, and institutional climate, the section related to assessment is, by necessity, more general. This handbook is not intended to standardize assessment and evaluation processes because Honors Programs and Honors Colleges value their differences and flexibility. Its purpose is to provide some guidelines to help deans and directors establish assessment and evaluation procedures that are effective for their individual programs or colleges. The monograph addresses the difference between Honors consultants and Honors external reviewers as well as the benefits derived from both sets of specialists. Very important to Honors directors and deans is the section concerning the external review process. This section provides Honors administrators explicit information on the various aspects of an external review. It details what administrators must do prior to a site visit, the goals and schedule for a successful site visit, and expectations subsequent to the site visit. The last section before the appendices offers directions for those who are interested in becoming an NCHC-recommended Site Visitor. Finally, the monograph contains appendices with several lists, examples, and models that can be useful to Honors administrators in the development of procedures for evaluating their Honors Program or Honors College.

Although it is the largest national organization concerned with Honors education, the National Collegiate Honors Council at present does not serve as an accrediting body for Honors Programs and Honors Colleges. NCHC-recommended Site Visitors and consultants have a wide range of Honors experience. Site visitors also have completed a Faculty Institute for Site Visitor Training.

ACKNOWLEDGMENTS

The appendices to this monograph include Honors documents from a number of institutions, including our own. We would like to express our appreciation to our colleagues Larry Andrews (Kent State University), Richard Badenhausen (Westminster College of Salt Lake City), Bruce Fox (Northern Arizona University), Debra Hollman (University of Northern Colorado), Ada Long (University of Alabama, Birmingham), and Chris Willerton (Abilene Christian University). They graciously provided electronic copies of materials from their Honors Programs and Honors Colleges with permission to include them in this monograph.

We also would like to thank Ada Long (University of Alabama, Birmingham), Gary Bell (Texas Tech University), Charles "Jack" Dudley (Virginia Tech University), Jane Lawrence (University of California, Merced), Monica McAlpine (University of Massachusetts-Boston), Kathryn McDorman (Texas Christian University), Hallie Savage (Clarion University of Pennsylvania), and Arno Wittig (Ball State University). Through the years they have contributed to the development of the checklist for external Honors reviews that is discussed at length in Part Five of this monograph and contained in Appendix E.

In addition, we would like to thank the Honors Director whose external review report is contained, anonymously and in abbreviated form, in Appendix L.

Finally, we are grateful to Jeff Portnoy (Georgia Perimeter College) for his meticulous editing; to Lydia Lyons (Hillsborough Community College), George Mariz (Western Washington University), Richard Osberg (Santa Clara University), and Jean Sorensen (Grayson County College) for their valuable comments on the manuscript; and to Hallie Savage (Clarion University of Pennsylvania) and the other members of the NCHC Publications Board for their support and encouragement.

In recent years, institutions of higher education have experienced a strong pressure to demonstrate the effectiveness of their academic programs. Much of this movement has been externally driven by national organizations and agencies, and in some cases state legislatures, demanding visible and concrete accountability and verification that fiscal and human resources invested in educational institutions are being used in ways that result in high-quality education that positively impacts students. Furthermore, most accrediting agencies or other governing bodies are requesting that institutions assess student learning outcomes as a means to improve academic programs.

The outcomes assessment movement has become such an important component of comprehensive academic planning that many national accreditation agencies have mandated the implementation of assessment planning to general education, undergraduate majors and options, and graduate and professional school programs. Currently, more than twenty states require some form of outcomes assessment in higher education. Honors Programs and Honors Colleges are not exempt from the need for assessment and evaluation.

Assessment is the systematic, on-going, iterative process of monitoring a program or college to determine what is being done well and what needs improvement. The term "assessment" refers to the systematic gathering of information about component parts of the program to be evaluated. The evaluation process is broader than assessment and involves examining information about many components of the program or college being evaluated and making judgments about its worth and effectiveness.

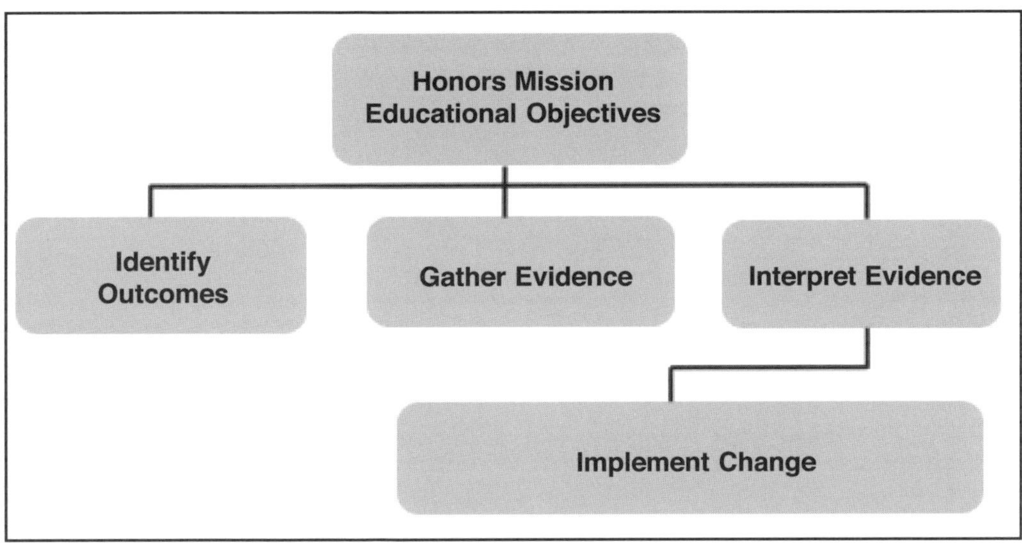

Figure 1. Methods of Assessment Effectiveness

Evaluation and assessment provide an opportunity for Honors Programs and Honors Colleges to demonstrate their strengths, address their weaknesses, generate institutional support, and gain outside validation of their accomplishments and goals. A thorough evaluation process begins with two interrelated phases. First, Honors Program or Honors College personnel conduct a self-study to clarify mission and objectives, to assess its success in attaining those objectives and fulfilling the mission, and to identify ways in which the effectiveness of Honors can be increased. Second, a team of experienced NCHC-recommended Site Visitors come to the institution for an on-site evaluation that is based on the program/college self-study report, the National Collegiate

Honors Council's "Basic Characteristics of a Fully Developed Honors Program," and (if applicable) NCHC's "Characteristics of a Fully Developed Honors College."

Peer review of academic programs is a widely accepted method for assessing curricular sequence, course development and delivery, and the effectiveness of faculty. Using external reviews is a helpful way of analyzing whether student achievements correlate appropriately with program or college goals and objectives. In numerous instances, recommendations initiated by skilled external reviewers have been instrumental in identifying program strengths and weaknesses, leading to substantial curricular and structural changes and improvements.

Success of Honors evaluation relies heavily on the collecting of reliable and valid data on student achievements and the variables to explain them. Assessment is effective when it is congruent with program objectives. It needs to be relevant, comprehensive, and fair. Honors administrators should use a variety of data-gathering methods designed to reflect the unique structure and goals of programs for Honors students. Assessment is defined as data-gathering strategies, analyses, and reporting processes that provide information that can be used to determine whether or not intended outcomes are being achieved. Assessment involves observing, describing, collecting, recording, and interpreting information. Evaluation uses assessment information to support decisions on maintaining, changing, or discarding instructional or programmatic practices. These strategies can inform the nature and extent of learning in an Honors Program and Honors College as well as facilitate curricular decision-making. When developing and implementing outcomes assessment strategies, Honors Programs and Honors Colleges should have at least one of three purposes in mind: to improve, to inform, and/or to prove. The results from an assessment process should provide information that can be used to determine whether or not intended outcomes are being achieved and how the programs can be improved. An assessment process should also be designed to inform faculty and other decision-makers about relevant issues that can impact the Honors Program or Honors College and student learning.

Assessment results or reports of external reviewers should be used in a timely manner to facilitate continuous programmatic improvements. Designing a feedback process is essential in all assessment plans because it offers Honors administrators and faculty the opportunity to use recent findings to incorporate changes necessary to improve the Honors Program or Honors College. Because Honors Programs and Honors Colleges vary widely, consulting with and evaluating Honors Programs and Colleges frequently present complex challenges.

In order to meet external demands for assessment implementation and to incorporate assessment into ongoing planning, Honors Programs and Honors Colleges should devise appropriate timetables for development and execution of assessment.

PART TWO. UNDERTAKING AN HONORS SELF-STUDY

Assessment should be ongoing and constant. Honors administrators should prepare an annual report that includes the successes as well as the inadequacies of the Program or College in that year. Recommended content of the annual report can be found in Appendix D. Developing extensive documentation annually is most useful for a variety of purposes including preparation for an external review of the program or college and even for such things as accreditation reviews of the institution. Annual reports should include both narrative sections and quantitative data. Generally, the annual report should include student statistics and graduate profiles as well as information on courses and faculty and activities undergone by the Honors Program or Honors College in the academic year. The report should be as detailed as possible including, for example, the names of students who graduated that year. It should include clear descriptions and goals utilizing multiple data sources: faculty, students, administrators, council/committee members, and advisors.

When such a report is generated annually, it becomes relatively simple to generate a self-study report. The report should be disseminated to all appropriate audiences in a timely fashion and with recommendations designed to encourage follow-through.

A self-study report is the major source of information about an Honors Program or Honors College. It defines the context in which the Honors Program or Honors College will be examined and is the focus of site reviewers' discussion during the visit. A self-study is a comprehensive report providing an in-depth analysis of the program or college's purposes, programs, services, resources, structures, and functions. It should include, of course, the successes of the program or college. It should also include areas that are in need of improvement. This honest assessment has the dual benefit of presenting a credible report and, perhaps more importantly, of achieving support from the institution to change or strengthen areas listed as weaknesses. Assessment for improvement can have the added benefit of showing external stakeholders the success of the Honors Program or Honors College in doing its job. Transparent assessment results can go a long way toward generating support for Honors education.

Honors administrators should bear in mind that, in planning its self-study, an Honors Program or Honors College should answer the following questions:

1.   What are this Honors Program's or Honors College's mission, goals, and objectives? How do they relate to those of the institution as a whole?
2.   Are these appropriate in its present time and place and for its present constituency?
3.   Are all the Honors activities consistent with its mission, goals, and objectives?
4.   Are its programs and activities designed to achieve its goals and objectives?
5.   Is there solid evidence that they are being achieved?
6.   Are the human, physical, and fiscal resources needed to achieve Honors Program or Honors College aims available now? Are they likely to be available for the foreseeable future?
7.   What else is there to know about the Honors Program or Honors College?
8.   What are the Honors Program's or Honors College's strengths and weaknesses?
9.   Who are the people to be interviewed?
10. What additional documents should be examined?

A self-study report must include a history of the program. At many institutions, the director serves a limited term. (The average is three years.) Institutional memory, therefore, depends on well-kept records. A self-study report provides one locus for keeping the history of the program or college. Any important or interesting information concerning its start may be included. Founding documents may also be included in the Appendices. Policy documents should include the mission and goals of the program and discussion about whether they are consistent with the educational mission of the institution.

The self-study report must include information about the organization of the program or college. What is the organizational structure? To whom does the administrator report? Is there provision for continuity of leadership? What kind of staff support does the program have? Is it only administrative or does it include advisement or development? It is also important for reviewers to understand how the program is governed. Is there an Honors Council or Committee? Is it advisory, policy-making, or both? Who at the institution are involved in governance? Is there a Student Honors Committee or Council? What are the functions of this student body? Finally, providing evidence of administrative support for Honors is important; evidence may include the budget, the physical facility of Honors, and participation by administrators in various Honors events.

Information about the Honors students is, of course, vital to a self-study report. The criteria for participation, statistics about the number of students participating in the program, a profile of the graduates and their successes, and other similar information can be helpful. A list of theses/

projects and other commendable achievements of the students should be included. In addition, the self-study should include information about recruitment, admission, and retention.

A report on the Honors curriculum is important. What courses have been offered? Who taught them? What were the enrollment figures for each course? Including a summative report of the evaluations also is valuable. The report should also include all of the activities and events that were sponsored by the program/college and any additional information that relates to Honors. An alumni survey, or other surveys such as about Honors housing, also should be included.

Incorporating the NCHC "Basic Characteristics of a Fully Developed Honors Program" or "Characteristics of a Fully Developed Honors College" can be of great value in the self-study process. In addition to forming a useful organizational framework, the characteristics help situate the program or college in the context of national guidelines.

PART THREE. ASSESSMENT

Honors courses in most Honors Programs and Honors Colleges maintain high academic expectations usually in small, highly interactive classes. Each Honors course should contribute to the educational objectives of the Honors Program or Honors College. Honors educators want students to demonstrate superior capabilities in essential lifelong skills including the abilities to read critically, express themselves effectively in speech and writing, reason ethically, engage in quantitative analysis, and think critically and creatively. Upon graduation, Honors students should have the ability to reflect critically on and integrate knowledge and issues within the broader societal and human context. They should also recognize their individual and collective responsibilities as citizens and leaders.

How do Honors Programs and Honors Colleges know that their goals are being met? Assessing for learning is a systematic and systemic process of inquiry. It is a core institutional process guided by questions about how well students learn what they are expected to learn—based on pedagogy; the design of curricula, co-curricula, and instruction; as well as other educational opportunities. By examining students' work, texts, performances, research, responses, and behaviors across the continuum of their learning, Honors administrators and faculty gain knowledge about the efficacy of their work.

This section is designed to assist Honors administrators as they assess Honors students' knowledge; understanding; abilities; habits of mind; and ways of thinking, knowing, and behaving. Assessment is not an easy task because how humans learn is complex. When students are asked how they learn, for example, one hears multiple answers including some of the following: repetition, practice, time, feedback, self-reflection, modeling, observation, and even through mistakes. Learning is a multidimensional process that differs from student to student.

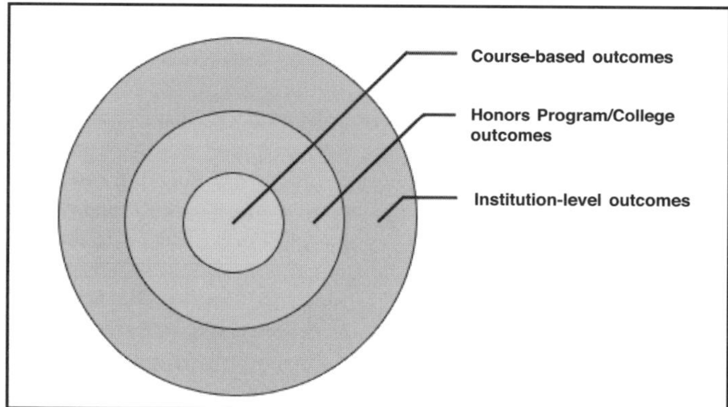

Figure 2. Collaboration among Levels of Outcomes

The assessment process should explore reasons why students are or are not achieving to assist those responsible in finding ways to improve the Honors Program or Honors College. Educational practices that need to be discussed include pedagogy, instructional design, curricular and co-curricular design, resources and tools, advising, and other educational opportunities such as internships or study abroad.

Assessment is most effective when it reflects an understanding of learning as multidimensional and revealed in performance through time. As mentioned earlier, learning is a complex process. It involves not only what students know but also what they can do with that knowledge. Assessment should reflect these understandings through a diverse array of methods, and it should be ongoing, not episodic.

Typically, Honors Programs and Honors Colleges record student achievement through a system of numbers and grades and, of course, the number of credit hours required to complete a program of Honors study. Some Programs and Colleges also complete qualitative evaluations to determine graduation with Honors and/or levels of Honors at graduation. Besides focusing on students' achievements in single courses, administrators also must focus on Honors-level learning through time as well as pay attention to the students' overall undergraduate education. Capturing the complexity of students' learning requires identifying or designing multiple methods of assessment. Combinations of quantitative and qualitative assessment methods add depth and breadth to interpretation of student learning. Quantitative methods place interpretive value on numbers–the number of right answers versus wrong answers. Qualitative methods place interpretative value on an individual's or group's performance. Honors faculty generally have a variety of methods for assessing student learning including student portfolios, capstone projects, performances, products or creations, visual representations, case studies, professional and disciplinary practices, team-based or collaborative projects, internships and service projects, and oral examinations.

Student portfolios are a collection of multiple kinds of student-generated texts stored electronically or in paper form. A portfolio provides evidence of a learner's achievements along the continuum of learning. Developments in technology now make it possible for students to create digital portfolios. This method of collection provides a longitudinal representation of learning through assignments, projects, and narrative self-analyses and self-reflection. Web folios, digital learning records, or electronic learning records are other current terms for this method.

Capstone projects may culminate in producing independent research or collaborative or professional projects at the end of the students' careers in Honors. This method provides evidence of how well students integrate, synthesize, and transfer learning. Senior theses or senior research projects are examples of capstone projects that provide opportunity for observers to assess students' mastery within a field of study, discipline, or profession.

These performances, products, or creations represent how Honors students interpret, express, and construct meaning. Traditionally, the arts' faculty have formatively assessed students' performances to provide them with immediate feedback that shapes their future performances. This approach provides not only students with immediate feedback but also faculty.

Representing learning visually through charting, graphing, or mapping provides students with alternative ways to show evidence of their learning, often a practice within disciplines such as mathematics and the sciences. Visual representation offers a way to assess how well students make connections or understand a concept. In addition, visual representation extends students' repertoire of making meaning, developing versatility in their responses to the different needs of audiences, contexts, and the purposes for communicating.

Case studies, often used in business programs, provide opportunity to assess students' problem-solving abilities. Professional or disciplinary practices also provide evidence of how well students transfer, apply, and integrate learning.

Team-based or collaborative projects are important because, with rare exception, humans work with other humans during most of their lives in a range of workplace, social, and community environments. Team-based or collaborative projects are direct methods that enable assessment of individuals' knowledge, understanding, behaviors, and attitudes, as well as their ability to work with others to achieve a final product or solve a problem.

Internships and service projects allow students to apply or transfer their cumulative knowledge. Authentic experiences become a direct method of assessment, providing opportunity for students to demonstrate the dimensions of their learning within the context of a real environment. A step beyond simulations, these direct methods assess how well students translate their cumulative learning into actual practice.

Often used at the end of an Honors Program or Honors College experience, oral examinations probe the dimensions of student learning. They offer opportunities for students to represent how well they integrate learning and apply it to solving a case study or problem, responding to guided questions, or making a presentation.

Besides the direct methods mentioned above, indirect methods may also be helpful in deepening interpretations of student learning. These methods focus on perceptions of student learning by asking students or others to respond to a series of questions. Indirect methods complement direct methods rather than substitute for them. Some examples of indirect methods include focus groups, interviews, and surveys and questionnaires. (See Appendix J for a sample senior exit packet and Appendix K for alumni surveys.)

PART FOUR. HONORS CONSULTANTS

Honors consultants are useful agents in assisting Honors administrators in a variety of ways. They are primarily useful in giving individual advice for a specific issue rather than general information that may be useful to many Honors Programs and Honors Colleges. They can target particular problems or questions. External reviewers, on the other hand, do not target specific issues or questions in isolation. They evaluate the whole program or college within the contexts of the institution and national norms. They generally use the "Basic Characteristics of a Fully Developed Honors Program" or "Characteristics of a Fully Developed Honors College" as the appraisal instrument. The "Basic Characteristics of a Fully Developed Honors Program" (Appendix A) were crafted by the NCHC Honors Evaluation Committee and approved by the NCHC Executive Committee on March 4, 1994. The "Characteristics of a Fully Developed Honors College" (Appendix B) were proposed by the Ad Hoc Task Force on Honors Colleges. The Task Force's draft was modified slightly and then approved by the NCHC Executive Committee on June 25, 2005.

Consultants can situate individual Honors practices within the national Honors context. They can provide outside perspective with which to analyze the needs of the Honors Program or Honors College. Consultants can assist with particular issues that concern that Program or College.

Each Honors Program and Honors College is unique, with a distinctive mission, history, leadership style, capabilities, resource availability, culture, and set of challenges. The goal of NCHC consultants is to respond to the specific need of the individual Honors Program or Honors College. Their advice may range from facilitating custom-designed on-campus workshops to serving as technical advisors to a review team.

Consultants may be invited to visit a campus to assist with targeted issues. Consultations and workshops can be especially beneficial if there is sufficient need for training on a particular topic. Consultants can help with such issues as the following:

> planning curriculum;
> teaching strategies for faculty;
> evaluating or redesigning courses;
> deterring, detecting, and dealing with plagiarism;
> designing distance learning;
> developing leadership skills; and
> designing a mentoring system.

Campuses should contact a consultant directly to discuss their interests and consulting needs. Arrangements regarding the length and structure of a consultation contract, as well as fees, are negotiated individually between the institution and consultant. Normally campuses cover travel costs plus an honorarium.

Honors administrators may take advantage of the Consultants Center held during the annual NCHC Conference. Experienced Honors deans and directors volunteer to be in session for at least one hour during the conference. The conference program lists these volunteers, their institutions, and their expertise. Conference attendees may stop by the Consultants Center to speak with one of the experienced volunteers and receive expert advice.

During the 2004 NCHC Conference, for example, twenty-seven Honors administrators participated in the Consultants Center. They gave advice on such topics as academic advising, extra-curricular programming, alumni relations, study abroad, curriculum development, scholarships, fundraising, and undergraduate research.

The use of the NCHC listserv is another valuable tool for receiving advice and sharing ideas. In recent years, the listserv has generated ideas ranging from the trappings of graduation ceremonies (the use of medallions or Honors cords and certificates of achievement) to becoming an Honors College.

PART FIVE. EXTERNAL REVIEWS

Part Five of this monograph provides a practical "nuts-and-bolts" discussion of the external review process rather than a theoretical approach to the matter; thus a veritable checklist provides the organizational theme.

OVERVIEW OF THE EXTERNAL REVIEW PROCESS

6 to 9 months before site visit	Develop budget; select site visitors; undertake self-study and develop supporting documentation; schedule key administrators, faculty, and students to meet with site visitors.
1 month before site visit	Deliver self-study and supporting documentation to site visitors.
Site Visit	Site visitors come to campus for two or three days.
1 month after site visit	Site visitors prepare and submit preliminary draft report and final report.
3 to 9 months after site visit	Honors administrator and others on campus respond to site visit report.

A. Before the Site Visit

1. Developing the Budget

An essential step is developing a program review budget to provide adequate resources for preparation of the materials that will be needed, honoraria and travel expenses for the site visitors, meals or other events on campus involving the site visitors and members of the campus community, and other miscellaneous expenses.

Although there is no prescribed scale for NCHC-recommended Site Visitors, an honorarium in the range of $750.00-$1,000.00 per day on campus is not unreasonable. If the review is part of a mandated institution-wide process, funding may be available from the Assessment Office or similar unit on campus. In many institutions, the Provost or President's Office can provide all or part of the funding for an external review, but the Honors director or dean may have to take the initiative to request these funds. (Significant side benefits of obtaining funding from the central administration are likely greater access to key administrators during the site visit and greater credibility attached to the final report from the site visitors because it is a centrally funded initiative.)

2. Selecting the Site Visitors and Scheduling the Visit

The selection of appropriate site visitors is important to a successful external review. The list of NCHC-recommended Site Visitors is available on the NCHC web page at <http://www.nchcHonors.org/consulting.htm>, or it may be obtained from the NCHC Headquarters Office at the University of Nebraska–Lincoln. Neither the NCHC Headquarters Office nor the Co-Chairs of the Assessment and Evaluation Committee may make recommendations of specific individuals from the list of recommended site visitors.

Although there obviously is no requirement that an Honors colleague from this list be used for a site visit, these recommended site visitors have extensive Honors experience and have completed at least one NCHC Faculty Institute for Site Visitor Training. (The requirements and process for becoming an NCHC-recommended Site Visitor are detailed in Part Six of this monograph.)

Why not just review documentation without an on-campus visit? On occasion, campus administrators may press for an external review based solely on a review of documents provided to the reviewer. Sometimes the reason is to reduce the cost to the institution—an increasing temptation in times of reduced budgets for higher education—but this is a "penny-wise, pound-foolish" approach. Another, more lamentable, motivation would be a desire to undertake only a minimal review that will gloss over Honors deficiencies. Whatever the reason underlying such an approach, neither of the authors of this monograph would agree to undertake a paper-only program review—nor would most other NCHC-recommended Site Visitors.

While documents can provide a wealth of background information about an Honors Program or Honors College, they cannot guarantee that actual practice matches the documentation. Only on-campus conversations with representatives of a wide range of Honors constituencies along with the opportunity to pursue follow-up questions can provide the information necessary to determine the health of the Honors endeavor at a particular institution.

Checking the actual campus experience against the documentation is by no means always disadvantageous to the institution. Interestingly enough, on-campus conversations can lead to a report that is more positive than a review of the documents alone might suggest. Exchanges with students, faculty, and administrators may well lead to the conclusion that what on paper appeared to be a problematic aspect of an Honors Program or Honors College is working extremely well in practice. If, however, the documentation attempts to overstate what is offered by Honors, the opposite result is to be anticipated.

How many site visitors? Although consulting for an Honors Program or Honors College frequently is undertaken by a single individual, an external review team should be made up of at least two and preferably three members. This strategy is preferable for several reasons. First, the experiences and perspectives of two or three experienced Honors colleagues are brought to bear on the Honors Program or Honors College under review. Second, in reading the materials provided in advance of the site visit, multiple readers will be more likely to pick up all of the necessary information: what is explicit in the documents and what is implicit or conspicuously absent. Third, it is extremely difficult, if not impossible, for one site visitor to understand fully every comment or nuance during the site visit process, so it is important for the site visitors to check the perceptions of other team members before and during the writing of the program review report. Fourth, the selection of site visitors from both similar and dissimilar institutions can broaden the perspectives contained in the report and work to the benefit of the Honors Program or Honors College. For all of these reasons, a number of NCHC-recommended Site Visitors, including the authors of this monograph, have concluded that it is neither feasible nor appropriate for a single individual to conduct a formal external review.

Who chooses the site visitors? The answer to this question will vary among institutions. If the Honors director or dean does not make the selection, providing a list of names to the person who will make the choice of site visitors is a good idea. On the NCHC web page, one can review brief resumés of potential site visitors. In addition to summarizing qualifications, these resumés list the institutions where NCHC-recommended Site Visitors have conducted site visits. Contacting some of these institutions is perfectly reasonable and quite common.

If more than two site visitors are coming to the campus, designating one of the site visitors to chair the visiting team is helpful. In any case, the site visitors will no doubt determine their responsibilities themselves.

Having enough advance notice in planning a site visit may allow time to meet informally with potential site visitors before making any selection. NCHC's annual fall conference or one of the regional Honors conferences can provide an excellent place for attendees to make such contacts and to visit with potential site visitors to determine whether they are likely to match the needs of the institution.

Who contacts the site visitors? The institution requesting the external review contacts the potential site visitors directly to determine availability, honoraria, and the like.

What to say to the site visitors? The site visitors who are selected will do their best to provide an objective evaluation of the strengths of the Honors Program or Honors College as well as any challenges that it faces, but they also will be advocates for Honors education. It is perfectly appropriate and indeed expected that the director or dean will enlist their support in the development of the Honors Program or Honors College. In addition to the written information that will be requested (see below), he or she should give as much background information as possible—as early as possible—in telephone conversations or e-mail exchanges. Why is the site visit being scheduled? What is the general campus culture with regard to Honors education? What are the strengths and weaknesses of the Honors Program or Honors College? Are there specific needs that the site visitors can address? Are there particular points of pride to call to their attention? Are there matters that need to be raised but which may be difficult, or imprudent, to include in the written materials? Are there political land mines on campus about which they need to be aware? Who are the allies of Honors education on the campus? Are there those who oppose Honors education, either overtly or covertly? What other things can help the site visitors appreciate the institutional environment for the Honors Program or Honors College?

How far in advance? Because preparing for an external review site visit, spending time on campus, and writing the report are time-consuming activities, most site visitors by necessity limit themselves to one or two external reviews in any given semester. For this reason, contacting potential site visitors six months or more in advance of the preferred date of the visit is highly recommended.

3. Utilizing NCHC's Basic Characteristics as a Tool

NCHC's "Basic Characteristics of a Fully Developed Honors Program" (Appendix A) and, if applicable, "Characteristics of a Fully Developed Honors College" (Appendix B) provide an excellent starting point for the external review process. They provide a national framework for the work of preparing for the site visit and for the final report that will be prepared by the site visitors.

4. Materials to be Prepared

Before conducting external reviews, typically site visitors provide a list of requested materials and ask that all of the items be delivered at least one month before the actual site visit. Below is a list of materials requested by the authors of this monograph, along with some relevant questions and issues to be considered.

a. Please prepare a self-study containing a brief history of the Honors Program or Honors College. As part of your self-study, use of the National Collegiate Honors Council's "Basic Characteristics of a Fully Developed Honors Program" and (if applicable) "Characteristics of a Fully Developed Honors College" to help the site visitors assess how the Honors Program or Honors College meets or does not meet each of the characteristics. Please specify any short-term or long-term goals with regard to these characteristics.

b. Additional documents to be provided in advance of the visit if not included in the self-study report:

<u>1. college or university catalog</u>

The catalog contains a wealth of background information about the history, mission, and current operations of the institution for the site visitors to review before visiting the campus, and it also offers a view of the way in which the Honors Program or Honors College is presented to the public. How prominently is Honors featured in the catalog? How much detail is provided? Is the Honors administrator included in the list of key campus administrators? Does the index direct readers to all information about the Honors Program or Honors College?

<u>2. mission statement of the Honors Program or Honors College</u>

What is the formal mission statement of the Honors Program or Honors College? How does it fit with the overall mission of the institution? Has the mission statement been approved by the central administration at the institution? How well do the current operations mesh with and fulfill the mission statement?

<u>3. Honors Program or Honors College strategic plan [if applicable]</u>

Although not every academic institution has undertaken strategic planning, increasing numbers of colleges and universities are doing so. Honors should be an integral part of the institution's strategic plan, and Honors administrators should utilize the strategic planning process to position themselves in the institution for future growth and development. If the Honors Program or Honors College has a strategic plan, it should be provided. In addition, documentation of progress made toward strategic goals should be part of the materials.

<u>4. position descriptions for Honors director or dean and Honors office staff</u>

The amount of detail in the descriptions of positions will vary among institutions, but the site visitors should have a general idea of the responsibilities of all of the Honors administrators and staff with whom they will visit.

<u>5. recruiting materials for the college or university in general and the Honors Program or Honors College in particular</u>

How does the institution recruit new students? How prominently is the Honors Program or Honors College featured in general recruiting materials? How accurate is the information, and how frequently is it updated? What specific materials relate to potential Honors students? Who is responsible for their content, and how are they utilized?

<u>6. Honors Program or Honors College budget for the past five years, including salary for the Honors director and an average salary figure for assistant or associate deans and directors across campus</u>

One crucial element of the success of any Honors Program or Honors College is the budget. The site visitors should be provided as much detailed budget information as possible. If the number of Honors students has grown, has the Honors budget increased over the same time period? If an institution is expecting its Honors Program or Honors College to operate on the proverbial shoestring, questions certainly will be raised during the site visit and in the final written report. These questions sometimes result in positive changes in the budget situation.

Honors administrators should not be expected to work for nothing or at a rate well below that provided for comparable academic administrators on campus. Having comparative data allows the site visitors one measure by which to gauge the support being provided by the institution's central administration.

A telling question during some site visits can be to ask higher-level administrators who say that Honors education is a high institutional priority to compare the size of the Honors budget with the amount spent by the institution for under-prepared students.

<u>7. Honors Program or Honors College policies and procedures documents</u>

Every Honors Program or Honors College operates under some sort of rules and procedures. Faculty and students benefit if these rules and procedures are codified and made readily available. (By way of example only, the Honors College polices and procedures from Oklahoma State University are included in Appendix F.)

Reviewing the policies and procedures document will give the site visitors an understanding of the legal structure of the Honors Program or Honors College, information that is quite important in preparing for the time that will be spent on campus during the review process. Thoughtful policies and procedures are a definite plus in the review process as long as the reviewers verify that actual practice is consistent with the stated policies. On the other hand, however, if the site visitors conclude that policies are not followed, this fact almost certainly will be raised as a concern in the final written report.

<u>8. Honors Program or Honors College annual reports for past five years</u>

Annual reports are quite important in documenting the history and success of an Honors Program or Honors College. Because Honors administrators at many institutions serve for relatively short periods, sometimes just three or four years, the risk of losing Honors institutional memory is great. Even at institutions where the Honors director or dean has served for many years, having an archive of past annual reports is extremely helpful when questions arise.

Certainly no one model exists for an annual report, but many institutions' annual Honors reports contain the vast majority of information that is included in this checklist for an external review, thereby making a self-study a far less onerous undertaking than if all of the information had to be sought out from musty files and sketchy memories. (See Appendix D for suggested contents of an annual report.)

Annual Honors reports are a valuable resource for external reviews, but this is not the only value of these reports. They become important documents for the institution's decennial accreditation review. They are useful for publicizing the successes of the Honors Program or Honors College and the Honors students at the institution. Copies should be distributed widely on campus to key administrators, either in hard copy or as electronic files. Placing a read-only file containing the annual report on the web page is a way to make the information available to alumni and others in an off-campus audience.

If the Honors Program or Honors College does not already compile a complete report each year, now is the time to start.

<u>9. listing and description of Honors courses offered in past five years (if not included in annual reports)</u>

Site visitors will want to know about the Honors courses that are available to Honors students. Is there a good selection of courses, or do the offerings appear to be tailored only to a segment of the student body? Has there been any innovation in the curriculum, or has it remained essentially the same during the last five years? How are these courses described?

<u>10. longitudinal data of Honors course offerings and student participation in the Honors Program or Honors College during the past five years (if not included in annual reports)</u>

The longitudinal data requested under this item provide an additional dimension for evaluation. For example, if the number of Honors students has increased during this time span, has there been a corresponding increase in the number of Honors courses? Unfortunately some institutions assert pressure to increase numbers in Honors without providing necessary resources to serve the additional Honors students who have been recruited. This scenario certainly will be a flag to the site visitors well before they reach the campus for the on-site visit.

<u>11. participation in NCHC and Regional Honors Council activities (if not included in annual reports)</u>

Quality Honors Programs and Honors Colleges do not operate in a vacuum. Active participation in NCHC, regional Honors organizations, and state Honors organizations provides perspective not available on one's own campus. While attendance at national and regional conferences is a good start, the next step is making presentations at these conferences and becoming involved with Honors colleagues in committee work and other aspects of the larger national Honors community.

How frequently does the institution participate in these conferences? Is the participation passive or active? What is the range of participation from the Honors Program or Honors College? Are individuals from the campus active on committees and leadership positions? What other connections have been established with off-campus Honors colleagues?

12. evaluation materials used for Honors classes

How does the Honors Program or Honors College evaluate Honors classes? What instruments are used? How is the information gained from these evaluations used? Is prompt feedback provided to the faculty? If problems are identified, how are they addressed? Are course evaluation results made available to Honors students as part of the Honors advising process?

13. evaluation materials used for Honors advising

How does the Honors Program or Honors College evaluate Honors advising? What instruments are used? How is the information gained from evaluation used? Is prompt feedback provided to the Honors advisors? How does the evaluation process contribute to improved Honors advising?

14. Honors Program or Honors College assessment approaches and results

Does the Honors Program or Honors College have an overall assessment plan? If so, how it is structured? What is assessed, and how is this assessment undertaken? What are the results of the assessment activities? How are these results reported on campus?

15. information about any scholarships or scholarship programs dedicated to Honors students

What scholarships does the Honors Program or Honors College provide? Is Honors Program or Honors College participation taken into account in the awarding of other scholarships?

In addition to scholarships for current Honors students, what role if any does the Honors Program or Honors College play in identifying students who may wish to compete for prestigious national and international scholarships (Rhodes, British Marshall, Truman, Goldwater, Fulbright, etc.) and in assisting these students as they prepare for competition? At some institutions, the Honors Program or Honors College has primary responsibility in this area; at others, two or more campus units cooperate. Whatever the arrangement, it is only natural to assume that Honors students are likely to be among those who compete for and receive such recognition.

16. information about links between Honors and overseas programs

Are Honors students encouraged to study abroad? If the Honors Program or Honors College is not the primary point of contact for students interested in international study, does it have a close working relationship with the office on campus that is responsible? Are Honors courses that incorporate international study offered? How may study abroad be counted toward the academic requirements of the Honors Program or Honors College?

17. guidelines or manuals for thesis or creative projects

If an Honors thesis is required, what guidelines or materials are provided to Honors students before they undertake their Honors thesis work?

18. information about any privileges that Honors students receive

What fringe benefits are earned by Honors students? Are they entitled to priority enrollment, as is the case at many NCHC institutions? If so, how does priority enrollment work? Is an Honors residence hall option available? If so, what are the criteria for Honors housing eligibility? Do Honors students have extended library checkout privileges? Is there an Honors library, computer laboratory, or student lounge? Do Honors students receive discounts or free admission for campus cultural events? What other benefits accrue to Honors students?

<u>19. information on role, if any, of the Honors Program or Honors College in promotion and tenure decisions</u>

Just as Honors administrators should not be expected to work for nothing, faculty who are successful in Honors education should receive credit in terms of promotion and tenure in the overall context of institutional policies on these matters. Does Honors matter for promotion and tenure? How does the Honors Program or Honors College contribute to the process?

If the Honors Program or Honors College has its own faculty lines, what are the standards for promotion and tenure?

If the Honors director or dean has not already attained the rank of professor, how is success in Honors administration and teaching, if applicable, taken into account in the requirements for advancement in faculty rank?

<u>20. structure of and administrative policies concerning the student Honors organization</u>

Does the institution have a student Honors organization or organizations? How is this organization structured? What role does it play? Does this organization contribute to the governance of the Honors Program or Honors College? How many students actively participate in the organization?

<u>21. facilities of the Honors Program or Honors College</u>

Honors space is an important feature of any Honors Program or Honors College. The office space should be adequate and attractive. It should be located centrally and not relegated to an out-of-the way location. Ideally, Honors classrooms and seminar rooms should be part of the Honors space, as should computer facilities, informal gathering space, study rooms, or other space for Honors students. The reviewers will provide their assessment of the space assigned to the Honors Program or Honors College.

B. During the Visit

This section deals with the logistics of scheduling the site visit. Scheduling all of the appointments and meetings falls to the on-campus person responsible for the external review, typically the Honors director or dean. A few preliminary comments may be of assistance.

1. Goals for the Site Visit

The goals for the site visit should be clear. While these goals should have been communicated to the site visitors well in advance of their arrival on campus, it is a good idea to repeat them when the site visitors arrive at the institution. The purpose of the external review is to help validate the strengths of the Honors Program or Honors College, point out ways to remedy possible weaknesses, and assist with meeting goals.

2. Developing an Appropriate Schedule

A two-day site visit is a fairly typical arrangement although on occasion three days are involved. Site visitors probably will arrive late in the day before the first full on-campus day begins. If travel arrangements permit, an entrance interview can be scheduled for the evening of arrival, perhaps including a meal.

Site visitors expect that the on-campus days will be proverbial treadmill experiences with little down time. A typical day starts with a working breakfast, a series of meetings in the morning, a working lunch, more meetings in the afternoon, and frequently a working dinner. Because students often find evenings more agreeable to their schedules, a meeting with students on the first evening after dinner is not uncommon.

If possible, Honors students may escort the site visitors from meeting to meeting when they are scheduled in different locations. The informal conversations with students in this setting can be quite informative and provide additional context for the overall site visit.

Site visitors definitely need some time each day to confer among themselves, so providing time in the schedule for about an hour of visitors' discussion time at a private location is an excellent idea. Making such arrangements also provides the opportunity, if necessary, to meet with individuals not already on the schedule or for the site visitors to take the initiative to visit a campus location that has been called to their attention.

If travel arrangements permit, the exit interview should take place on the morning of the site visitors' departure from campus. Otherwise, it typically will be the last item of the final day of the visit.

Unless a specific reason not to do so exists, the Honors director or dean typically is not present during most of the meetings scheduled for the site visitors.

After the schedule of meetings has been completed, it should be communicated to the site visitors and include at least the following information: schedule of meetings, location of those meetings, names and titles of the persons expected to be in attendance, and the relationship of those persons to the Honors Program or Honors College. Of course complete information will not be possible for open meetings with Honors faculty and Honors students, but the site visitors will appreciate receiving in advance as much detailed information as possible about the schedule for the site visit.

3. Meetings with the Site Visitors

The list of meetings provided below is a starting point, but almost always the Honors director or dean will add to this list based on the particulars of the institution. Because many of the individuals listed below have appointment schedules that are arranged weeks or months in advance, contact should be made with them as early as possible to be certain that they will be available to meet with the site visitors.

While personal styles among site visitors naturally will vary, that members of the visiting team take extensive notes during these meetings is fairly common. The tone of the sessions, however, typically is that of a conversation among colleagues rather than that of a formal meeting.

The list of meetings does not include visits to individual Honors classes. The authors' own experience has led them to conclude that their presence in a class introduces an artificial element that most likely makes the session non-representative of the regular class experience. This is not to say that an Honors director or dean never should schedule such a meeting, but visiting classes is not essential to a valid external review process.

<u>a. college or university president and the chief academic officer of the college or university</u>

It is important that the site visitors meet with the top administrators of the college or university. The preferable arrangement would be separate sessions with the president and the chief academic officer, but a combined meeting may be the campus norm.

This time with the top administrators allows the site visitors to gauge the level of administrative commitment to Honors education, to explore the goals of the president and chief academic officer, to ask questions and raise points of concern, and to be advocates for Honors education. As noted above, the Honors director or dean should have informed the site visitors about any political land mines on campus so that they do not inadvertently cause harm during these conversations. On the other hand, if difficult questions need to be asked, it is extremely helpful if the Honors director or dean has provided the site visitors with complete background information.

b. vice provost for academic affairs

At a large institution, the vice provost for academic affairs may be the key contact person for the Honors director or dean on a day-to-day basis. If this structure exists, a separate meeting should be scheduled with the person in this position.

c. deans of undergraduate colleges involved with the Honors Program or Honors College

When an institution has multiple undergraduate colleges, the deans of these colleges can be key allies in the Honors effort, or they can be major stumbling blocks. Discussions with these deans can both allow interaction among them to share their Honors success and give the site visitors an opportunity to provide examples of how similar undergraduate colleges elsewhere cooperate with and profit from the Honors Program or Honors College.

Depending on the nature of the institution, another meeting that may be profitable is one with department heads or chairs of departments actively involved with Honors education and with departments that should be involved but for some reason are not actively contributing to the overall Honors effort at the institution.

d. Honors Program or Honors College director or dean

Ample time should be scheduled for the site visitors to meet privately with the Honors director or dean. In many instances the schedule includes an entrance interview, an extended meeting during the site visit, and an exit interview.

e. Honors office staff

The site visitors should meet with all key Honors office staff members. If the staff is small, individual meetings can be scheduled. If the staff is large, grouping staff members with similar responsibilities may be necessary.

f. open meeting with faculty for Honors courses [limited to these faculty]

To say that the faculty who teach Honors classes are absolutely crucial to a successful Honors Program or Honors College is to belabor the obvious. Meeting with these faculty in an informal setting is extremely helpful for the site visitors, so this meeting should be scheduled at a time to facilitate a good turnout.

The meeting with Honors faculty frequently becomes a discussion forum that covers a wide range of topics and points of view. In addition to discussing Honors at their own institution, faculty often inquire of the visitors about other institutions' Honors Programs and Honors Colleges.

g. faculty and student Honors committees

Faculty and student committees involved with the governance of the Honors Program or Honors College make up another important component of Honors education. Members of these committees typically have more information and insight into the complexities of Honors operations than do other faculty and students, and they often have realistic suggestions for bettering Honors education. If they really are important to the Honors Program or Honors College, that fact should be apparent to the site visitors. If they are essentially window dressing, that fact also can become apparent during these meetings.

<u>h. open meeting with Honors students [limited to these students]</u>

At least an hour should be built into the site visitors' schedule to allow them to meet informally with Honors students in an open forum setting limited to these students. The meeting should be publicized well in advance to Honors students; a reminder shortly before the meeting should follow. During this meeting, leaders of the Honors student organization and Honors student committee who will have met with or will meet with the site visitors separately should take care not to dominate the discussions so that the site visitors will have an opportunity to interact with a wide range of Honors students to hear their opinions.

As already noted above, scheduling this meeting on the evening of the first full day of the site visit often leads to the greatest participation, but of course this may not be the best time for every institution. Serving food at the meeting provides an extra incentive for students to attend. The idea is to provide a comfortable, informal setting at a time convenient for these students.

<u>i. others thought appropriate by those responsible for the review process</u>

The meetings included above in this checklist are essential, but the list is by no means exhaustive. Depending on the situation at the institution, other key players may be identified to meet with the site visitors. Examples might include the registrar, admissions director, scholarships director, public relations director, and housing director, just to name a few. If additional people on campus are important to the current success and plans for the future of the Honors Program or Honors College, the site visitors would like to meet with them.

C. After the Site Visit

While the Honors director or dean can breathe a sigh of relief that the visit has been concluded, the site visitors now must move into even higher gear to prepare the final written report that will conclude their part of the external review process. Depending on the complexity of the situation, the amount of time required to write the formal report may vary from several weeks to six weeks or more. Typically, the report is completed within a month after the visit to the campus.

1. Preliminary Site Visitors Report

The site visitors will confer extensively about the draft written report, frequently exchanging several drafts by e-mail or FAX before they are satisfied with the report. After the draft report has been completed, many site visitors will provide a confidential preliminary copy of the report to the Honors director or dean with the request that he or she indicate any factual errors such as misspelled names, incorrect titles, or misperceptions of verifiable facts. To speed the process along, the preliminary report typically is transmitted as an electronic file attachment to e-mail.

Reviewing the draft is not an opportunity to attempt to dissuade the site visitors from their reasoned positions reflected in the report, but the Honors dean or director should not hesitate to raise any points of concern. If the report threatens to detonate the political land mines mentioned above, the Honors director or dean can suggest why and how they might be avoided.

A point worth making here is that no site visit to a campus can completely comprehend every facet of an Honors Program or Honors College. In essence, it amounts to a two-day snapshot of Honors life at the institution, and that along with the written materials they have received is all that the site visitors may honestly reflect in their written report.

2. Final Report

After reviewing the comments and suggestions of the Honors director or dean made in response to a review of the preliminary report, the site visitors will complete their final written report, thus concluding the external review process. The chair of the visiting team will transmit the final written report along with a cover letter to each recipient. Copies of the report usually are sent to the president, the chief academic officer, and the Honors director or Honors dean. If others should receive a copy, the chair of the site visit team can prepare and transmit additional copies. Frequently, the chair will send both electronic copies as e-mail attachments and hard copies of the report via the U.S. Postal Service.

3. Utility of the Final Report

Receipt of the final external review report on campus should not be the end of the process because it can be of benefit to the Honors Program or Honors College in many ways. A few examples are provided below.

The final report can and should be disseminated widely on campus. Obvious recipients are key campus administrators to whom the report was not transmitted by the chair of the site visit team, members of the faculty and student Honors committees, officers of the student Honors organization, and key Honors alumni. Wide dissemination of the report provides a solid basis for discussions with and among the recipients.

Assuming that the report is a generally positive one, a copy or key excerpts might be sent to the office on campus responsible for the institution's public relations. If appropriate, direct communication with the commercial media can provide positive publicity for the Honors Program or Honors College. The report, of course, represents the opinions of the site visitors, not those of the National Collegiate Honors Council as an organization.

A copy of the report should be filed for use during the next external review as well as for the decennial institutional accreditation review.

If areas of concern are noted in the report, this fact and the recommendations of the site visitors can be a springboard for discussions on campus. In many cases, Honors directors and deans have used the final report to strengthen Honors education in relatively short order. Even if immediate positive changes are not forthcoming, the final report may be of significant value at a later date, either as new high-level campus administrators come into office or when current administrators have additional resources. Using the final report as one measuring rod for progress has been an effective approach at many colleges and universities. A successful Honors director or dean always should have a wish list for Honors improvements, and the final report can be evidence of the appropriateness of items on that wish list.

If the final report does not fully address the strengths or needs of the Honors Program or Honors College, the director or dean may wish to write a follow-up document that responds to the site visitors' report. This commentary could circulate with the report to provide additional perspective to the readers.

The National Collegiate Honors Council must have a substantial number of site visitors it has trained and can recommend, in part because the Honors Programs and Honors Colleges that are members of the NCHC differ widely. Without a sufficient number of site visitors, NCHC cannot address the needs of its varied constituents. In addition, scheduling a site visit becomes easier with more choices.

The NCHC Headquarters Office maintains and makes available a list of NCHC-recommended Site Visitors. This list may be found on the NCHC website in addition to specific professional information about each site visitor to facilitate member institutions in the selection of appropriate reviewers.

An individual who is interested in becoming an NCHC-recommended Site Visitor must be a current NCHC institutional representative or individual professional member of NCHC and must have attended three out of the last five national conferences, including the conference at which his or her application is considered. The individual also must have successfully completed an NCHC Institute for Site Visitor Training. These Institutes generally are offered every other year and have been held in Brooklyn (2000), Chicago (2002), and Albuquerque (2004). A 2006 Institute is being planned at the NCHC Headquarters Office in Lincoln, Nebraska. To be considered, an applicant must submit an application form, abbreviated curriculum vitae limited to Honors and assessment/evaluation activities, the names and addresses of three relevant professional references (at least two must be from institutions other than the applicant's own home institution), and a one-page statement of the applicant's views on the role of a site visitor.

NCHC's Assessment and Evaluation Committee reviews the application materials and submits the names of persons recommended as new site visitors to the Executive Committee, which has the authority to direct the addition of names to the list of recommended site visitors.

To remain on the list, site visitors must be current NCHC institutional representatives or individual professional members of NCHC, have attended three out of the last five national conferences (on a rolling basis), update the required information forms for the web page by January 31 of each year (including the institutions for which they have conducted site visits in the previous calendar year), and have conducted at least one site visit or have attended an NCHC Institute for Site Visitor Training in the preceding six years.

Neither the chair nor co-chair of the Assessment and Evaluation Committee, nor any officer or employee of NCHC, may recommend specific site visitors but shall instead refer those asking for such information to the list of recommended site visitors. Two exceptions to this policy are permitted when (1) the chair or co-chair, or officer or employee of NCHC, has been selected as a site visitor himself or herself and is asked to suggest names for additional members of the site visit team or (2) recommendations are made according to policies approved by the Executive Committee in consultation with the Assessment and Evaluation Committee.

The NCHC-recommended Site Visitors are a group of experienced Honors administrators and educators. Individually, each NCHC-recommended Site Visitor brings years of experience, knowledge, and skills to Honors Programs and Honors Colleges. Collectively, these people offer familiarity with a range of Program or College types, cultures, and geographic locations. Representing a wide range of expertise, these people provide individual and group consultation to institutions working on a comprehensive review of their Honors Program or Honors College. They assist Honors Programs and Honors Colleges as they align their goals with those articulated in the "Basic Characteristics of a Fully Developed Honors Program" and the "Characteristics of a Fully Developed Honors College. They situate individual Honors Programs and Honors Colleges within the national Honors context and provide outside perspective to analyze Honors Program or Honors College needs. Institutional representatives should select site visitors whose expertise corresponds to the needs and interests of the institution.

A successful Site Visit Team is one that not only respects and follows ethical standards regarding conflict of interest, personal conduct, and communication and confidentiality issues, but also conscientiously prepares itself by studying in advance the self-study document, background materials, and other information received about the Honors Program or Honors College. Team members are expected to contribute to a thoughtful assessment of the Honors Program or Honors College, measuring the validity of the image projected in the self-study document and drawing upon the insights gained by the team from on-site contacts and discussions.

APPENDIX A

BASIC CHARACTERISTICS OF A FULLY DEVELOPED HONORS PROGRAM
(Approved by the NCHC Executive Committee on March 4, 1994)

No one model of an honors program can be superimposed on all types of institutions. However, there are characteristics that are common to successful fully developed honors programs. Listed below are those characteristics, although not all characteristics are necessary for an honors program to be considered a successful and/or fully developed honors program.

* A fully developed honors program should be carefully set up to accommodate the special needs and abilities of the undergraduate students it is designed to serve. This entails identifying the targeted student population by some clearly articulated set of criteria (e.g., GPA, SAT score, a written essay). A program with open admission needs to spell out expectations for retention in the program and for satisfactory completion of program requirements.

* The program should have a clear mandate from the institutional administration ideally in the form of a mission statement clearly stating the objectives and responsibilities of the program and defining its place in both the administrative and academic structure of the institution. This mandate or mission statement should be such as to assure the permanence and stability of the program by guaranteeing an adequate budget and by avoiding any tendency to force the program to depend on temporary or spasmodic dedication of particular faculty members or administrators. In other words, the program should be fully institutionalized so as to build thereby a genuine tradition of excellence.

* The honors director should report to the chief academic officer of the institution.

* There should be an honors curriculum featuring special courses, seminars, colloquia, and independent study established in harmony with the mission statement and in response to the needs of the program.

* The program requirements themselves should include a substantial portion of the participants' undergraduate work, usually in the vicinity of 20% to 25% of their total course work and certainly no less than 15%.

* The program should be so formulated that it relates effectively both to all the college work for the degree (e.g., by satisfying general education requirements) and to the area of concentration, departmental specialization, pre-professional or professional training.

* The program should be both visible and highly reputed throughout the institution so that it is perceived as providing standards and models of excellence for students and faculty across the campus.

* Faculty participating in the program should be fully identified with the aims of the program. They should be carefully selected on the basis of exceptional teaching skills and the ability to provide intellectual leadership to able students.

* The program should occupy suitable quarters constituting an honors center with such facilities as an honors library, lounge, reading rooms, personal computers, and other appropriate decor.

* The director or other administrative officer charged with administering the program should work in close collaboration with a committee or council of faculty members representing the colleges and/or departments served by the program.

*   The program should have in place a committee of honors students to serve as liaison with the honors faculty committee or council who must keep them fully informed on the program and elicit their cooperation in evaluation and development. This student group should enjoy as much autonomy as possible conducting the business of the committee in representing the needs and concerns of all honors students to the administration, and it should also be included in governance, serving on the advisory/policy committee as well as constituting the group that governs the student association.

*   There should be provisions for special academic counseling of honors students by uniquely qualified faculty and/or staff personnel.

*   The honors program, in distinguishing itself from the rest of the institution, serves as a kind of laboratory within which faculty can try things they have always wanted to try but for which they could find no suitable outlet. When such efforts are demonstrated to be successful, they may well become institutionalized, thereby raising the general level of education within the college or university for all students. In this connection, the honors curriculum should serve as a prototype for things that can work campus-wide in the future.

*   The fully developed honors program must be open to continuous and critical review and be prepared to change in order to maintain its distinctive position of offering distinguished education to the best students in the institution.

*   A fully developed program will emphasize the participatory nature of the honors educational process by adopting such measures as offering opportunities for students to participate in regional and national conferences, Honors Semesters, international programs, community service, and other types of experiential education.

*   Fully developed two-year and four-year honors programs will have articulation agreements by which honors graduates from two-year colleges are accepted into four-year honors programs when they meet previously agreed-upon requirements.

APPENDIX B

CHARACTERISTICS OF A FULLY DEVELOPED HONORS COLLEGE
(Approved by the NCHC Executive Committee on June 25, 2005)

An honors educational experience can occur in a wide variety of institutional settings. When institutions establish an honors college or embark upon a transition from an honors program to an honors college, they face a transformational moment. No one model defines this transformation. Although not all of the following characteristics are necessary to be considered a successful or fully developed honors college, the National Collegiate Honors Council recognizes these as representative:

* A fully developed honors college should incorporate the relevant characteristics of a fully developed honors program.

* A fully developed honors college should exist as an equal collegiate unit within a multi-collegiate university structure.

* The head of a fully developed honors college should be a dean reporting directly to the chief academic officer of the institution and serving as a full member of the Council of Deans, if one exists. The dean should be a full-time, 12-month appointment.

* The operational and staff budgets of fully developed honors colleges should provide resources at least comparable to other collegiate units of equivalent size.

* A fully developed honors college should exercise increased coordination and control of departmental honors where the college has emerged out of such a decentralized system.

* A fully developed honors college should exercise considerable control over honors recruitment and admissions, including the appropriate size of the incoming class. Admission to the honors college should be by separate application.

* An honors college should exercise considerable control over its policies, curriculum, and selection of faculty.

* The curriculum of a fully developed honors college should offer significant course opportunities across all four years of study.

* The curriculum of the fully developed honors college should constitute at least 20% of a student's degree program. An honors thesis or project should be required.

* Where the home university has a significant residential component, the fully developed honors college should offer substantial honors residential opportunities.

* The distinction awarded by a fully developed honors college should be announced at commencement, noted on the diploma, and featured on the student's final transcript.

* Like other colleges within the university, a fully developed honors college should be involved in alumni affairs and development and should have an external advisory board.

APPENDIX C

SELF-STUDY OUTLINE

1. Self-Study Based on *Basic Characteristics of a Fully Developed Honors Program* or *Characteristics of a Fully Developed Honors College*
2. History of the Honors Program/College
    Founding documents
    Policy documents
    Goals and objectives
3. Administrative design
    Director
        Tenure
        Duties
        Place in university administrative structure
    Staff
        Assistants/academic counselors
        Office and administrative staff
    Faculty Advising
    Advisory/Policy Council
        Authority
        Responsibilities
        Composition
    Budget
        Sources and basis
        Growth patterns
4. The Honors Student
    Criteria for participation
    Patterns of participation
    Success of students/alumni
    Financial aids
    Awards and recognition
    Community and identity
    Housing
    Student Honors association
    Participation of non-traditional students
    Transfer students
5. Recruitment and admissions
    Criteria
    Publications
    Modes of contact
    Retention
6. Curriculum
    Pattern
    Honors courses
    Research
    Other curricular opportunities
    Faculty appointments and status
    Enrollment
    Evaluation of courses and faculty
    Profile of Honors students
7. Survey results
    Faculty perception of program
    Honors student perception of program
    Honors alumni

Perception of program
Report of graduate study and support
Career status
Other surveys (Residence halls, non-traditional students, etc.)
8. Conclusions

APPENDIX D

THE HONORS ANNUAL REPORT

D-1. RECOMMENDED CONTENT FOR ANNUAL REPORT

1. Student statistics
   enrollment (total and new students)
   profiles of graduates
   majors/minors
   theses/projects titles
   grade point average data
   plans after graduation
2. Faculty statistics
3. Courses and evaluations
4. Budget
5. Lectures, Presentations, other events
6. Report of the Honors Student Advisory Council
7. Residence Hall Report (if applicable)
8. Goals
9. Sample newsletters, new recruitment materials, website, other publications
10. Conclusions

D-2. TABLE OF CONTENTS OF SAMPLE ANNUAL REPORT

Table of Contents of 2003-04 University of Alabama, Birmingham Annual Report

Narrative Summary, pages 2-7

APPENDICES
1. Departmental Honors Options
2. Bylaws and Membership of the Honors Program Advisory Board
3. National and International Involvement
4. Graduate, Professional and Career Choices of Honors Graduates
5. Post-Baccalaureate and Extramural Scholarships
6. Comparative Statistics of Pre-College and Post-College National Test Scores
7. Syllabus for 2003 Interdisciplinary Course
8. Lists of Honors Seminars, 2003-2004 and 2004-2005
9. Student Evaluation of Honors Program Interdisciplinary Course (Fall, 2003)
10. Retention Data of Honors Program
11. Comparative Lists of Students' ACT Scores, Honors GPAs, and UAB GPAs
12. Descriptions of Graduating Seniors
13. List of Honors Program Extracurricular Activities
14. Honors Program Committee Descriptions
15. Statistics on Racial Diversity
16. Disciplinary Affiliations of Current Students
17. Student Evaluation of Honors Program
18. Alumni/ae Evaluation of Honors Program and UAB
19. Extramural Support
20. Applications, Admissions, and Advising Data
21. Current Status of Scholarship Recipients
22. List of Students by Year, with High Schools and Majors
23. Special Information on Honors Students
24. Composition and Role of Honors Council
25. Responsibilities of Honors Program Administrators and Staff

26. Faculty Information Forms

2003-2004 Honors Program Publications, available on request
        Honors Program Student Newsletters (2)
        Alumni Newsletters (2)
        Honors Day Program
        2003-2004 Honors Program Student Handbook
        Journal of the National Collegiate Honors Council, III 1, III 2, IV 1, V 1
        Sanctuary 2003
        Reading Birmingham: City as Text© Explorations by Students of the UAB Honors Program

CHECKLIST FOR AN EXTERNAL REVIEW

This checklist has been developed by the authors, with the assistance of the Honors colleagues acknowledged in the Introduction, to guide Honors Program and Honors College deans and directors in preparing for an external review.

1. Please provide a self-study containing a brief history of the Honors Program or Honors College. As part of your self-study, use the National Collegiate Honors Council's "Basic Characteristics of a Fully Developed Honors Program" and (if applicable) "Characteristics of a Fully Developed Honors College" to help the site visitors assess how the Honors Program or Honors College meets or does not meet each of the characteristics. Please specify any short-term or long-term goals with regard to these characteristics.
2. Additional documents to be provided in advance of the visit if not contained in the self-study report:
   a. college (university) catalog
   b. mission statement of the Honors Program/College
   c. Honors Program (Honors College) strategic plan (if applicable)
   d. position descriptions for Honors director (dean) and Honors office staff
   e. recruiting materials for the college (university) in general and the Honors Program (Honors College) in particular
   f. Honors Program (Honors College) budget for the past five years, including salary for the Honors director and an average salary figure for assistant or associate deans and directors across campus
   g. Honors Program (Honors College) policies and procedures documents
   h. Honors Program (Honors College) annual reports for past five years
   i. listing and description of Honors courses offered in past five years (if not included in annual reports)
   j. longitudinal data of Honors course offerings and student participation in the Honors Program (Honors College) over the past five years (if not included in annual reports)
   k. participation in NCHC and Regional or State Honors Council activities (if not included in annual reports)
   l. evaluation materials used for Honors classes
   m. evaluation materials used for Honors advising
   n. Honors Program (Honors College) assessment approaches and results
   o. information about any scholarships or scholarship programs dedicated to Honors students
   p. information about links between Honors and overseas programs
   q. guidelines or manuals for thesis or creative projects
   r. information about any privileges (early enrollment, etc.) that Honors students receive
   s. information on role, if any, of the Honors Program (Honors College) in promotion and tenure decisions
   t. structure of and administrative policies concerning the student Honors organization
   u. facilities of the Honors Program (Honors College)
3. Conversations while on Campus
   a. college (university) president and the chief academic officer of the college (university)
   b. vice provost for academic affairs
   c. deans of undergraduate colleges involved with Honors program (Honors college)
   d. Honors Program (Honors College) director (dean)
   e. Honors Program (Honors College) office staff
   f. open meeting with faculty for Honors courses (limited to these faculty)
   g. faculty and student Honors committees
   h. open meeting with Honors students (limited to these students)
   i. others thought appropriate by those responsible for the review process

APPENDIX F

SAMPLE HONORS POLICIES AND PROCEDURES DOCUMENT

This policies and procedures document from The Honors College at Oklahoma State University is provided by way of example only.

Section 1 - The Honors College Mission Statement

Section 2 - Honors Councils

Section 3 - Admission, Continued Eligibility, and General Honors Award Requirements

Section 4 - College or Departmental Honors Award Requirements (Transcript Entry)

Section 5 - The Honors College Degree (Transcript Entry, Special Diploma)

SECTION 1. THE HONORS COLLEGE MISSION STATEMENT

The mission of The Honors College is to provide an enhanced and supportive learning environment for outstanding undergraduate students. This goal will be accomplished through the active involvement of faculty noted for their excellence in undergraduate teaching in small Honors sections of regular catalog courses, interdisciplinary Honors courses, special Honors seminars, and opportunities for research. The Honors College shall be a unit with its own budget with a Director who is administratively responsible to the Provost through the Associate Vice President for Academic Affairs. The Director shall work in close cooperation with a faculty University Honors Council and a University Student Honors Council to establish and review policies and procedures for The Honors Colleges. Consistent with these policies and procedures, The Honors College shall:

(1) disseminate information about Honors requirements, benefits, awards, and Honors College Degree recipients to prospective Honors students and other interested publics through direct communication, university publications, teleconferencing, and the news media;

(2) admit students to The Honors College, maintain records concerning their continued eligibility for The Honors College and their progress toward Honors College awards, and certify their Honors College awards and Honors College Degrees to the Registrar;

(3) provide special Honors academic advising through The Honors College Office by faculty and professional staff who themselves have earned Honors Program or Honors College degrees;

(4) encourage and coordinate the creation and scheduling of Honors sections of courses taught in the undergraduate colleges;

(5) develop, schedule, and budget interdisciplinary Honors courses and special Honors seminars using the HONR course prefix;

(6) promote Honors students' involvement in research that will culminate in a senior Honors thesis or project and public presentation of the research;

(7) facilitate communication within the OSU community among students, faculty, staff, and administration with regard to Honors matters;

(8) arrange special programs and events for the larger university community;

(9) equip and maintain The Honors College Study Lounge and computer facility in the Edmon Low Library; and

(10) participate fully in the activities of the National Collegiate Honors Council and the Great Plains Honors Council.

SECTION 2 - HONORS COUNCILS

2-1. UNIVERSITY HONORS COUNCIL. The University Honors Council shall be composed of the Director of The Honors College (ex officio chair of the Council) and seven faculty members whose budgeted assignment includes at least 0.25 FTE undergraduate instruction and who have a demonstrated interest in The Honors College, appointed by the Provost upon recommendation by the Deans of the OSU undergraduate colleges, as follows: Agricultural Sciences and Natural Resources (1), Arts & Sciences (2), Business Administration (1), Education (1), Engineering, Architecture and Technology (1), and Human Environmental Sciences (1). Members shall serve a term of three calendar years, beginning in the fall semester, and they may be reappointed.

Terms shall expire at the beginning of the fall semester of the years indicated below and every three years thereafter: Agricultural Sciences and Natural Resources, 1991; Arts & Sciences (#1), 1992; Arts & Sciences (#2), 1993; Business Administration, 1991; Education, 1992; Engineering, Architecture and Technology, 1991; and Human Environmental Sciences, 1993.

The University Honors Council shall be chaired by the Director of The Honors College and shall: (1) recommend to the Provost policy concerning course requirements and other criteria for Honors College awards; (2) represent the interests and concerns of faculty in the members' respective colleges concerning The Honors College; (3) represent The Honors College to the faculty of the members' respective colleges and serve as contact points for faculty; (4) serve, along with two members of the University Student Honors Council, as a committee to which students may appeal, in extraordinary circumstances, to be permitted to continue enrollment in Honors courses even though their cumulative grade point averages do not meet normal requirements under Honors College policy; (5) provide recommendations to the Director on any special situations concerning admission, etc., which may be referred to it by the Director; (6) review faculty proposals for Honors seminars and other special Honors courses that are to be funded through The Honors College; and (7) encourage and support faculty members seeking external funding through grants and contracts related to Honors College development.

2-2. UNIVERSITY STUDENT HONORS COUNCIL. The University Student Honors Council shall be composed of seven undergraduate students active in The Honors College, appointed by the Director of The Honors College upon recommendation by the Deans of the OSU undergraduate colleges, as follows: Agricultural Sciences and Natural Resources (1), Arts & Sciences (2), Business Administration (1), Education (1), Engineering, Architecture and Technology (1), and Human Environmental Sciences (1). Members shall serve a term of one calendar year, beginning in the fall semester, and they may be reappointed. The University Student Honors Council shall elect its own chairperson at the first meeting of the fall semester.

To serve on the University Student Honors Council, a student must have completed a minimum of fifteen Honors credit hours prior to appointment, have Oklahoma State University and cumulative grade point averages of at least 3.50, and continue to be an active participant in The Honors College as defined in Section 10-1, below. It is recommended that Deans nominate students who have completed the requirements for the General Honors Award or, if such students are not available, students who will complete the requirements for the General Honors Award at the conclusion of the semester in which they begin service on the University Student Honors Council.

The University Student Honors Council shall: (1) represent the interests and concerns of Honors students in the members' respective colleges; (2) represent The Honors College to the students of the members' respective colleges and serve as a contact point for student concerns with regard to The Honors College; (3) meet, as appropriate, in joint session with the faculty University Honors Council to discuss matters of common concern; (4) provide two of its members to serve with members of the University Honors Council as a committee to which students may appeal, in extraordinary circumstances, to be permitted to continue enrollment in Honors courses even though their grade point averages do not meet normal requirements under Honors College policy; (5) recommend and plan special events for Honors College students; and (6) make recommendations to the Director on any other matters concerning The Honors College.

**SECTION 3 - ADMISSION, CONTINUED ELIGIBILITY,
AND GENERAL HONORS AWARD REQUIREMENTS**

3-1. ADMISSION. Requirements for admission to The Honors College shall be as follows:

3-1-1. Entering Freshmen by ACT (SAT) Score and High School Grade Point Average.
Entering freshmen shall automatically be eligible by meeting the following criteria: a composite score of 27 or higher on the ACT (or comparable SAT score) and a high school grade point average of 3.75 or higher. (Weighted high school grade point averages certified by high schools may be used for this purpose.)

3-1-2. Entering Freshmen by Petition.

Entering freshmen who have an ACT score of 25-26 (or comparable SAT score) and a high school grade point average of 3.75 or higher, or who have an ACT score of 30 or higher (or comparable SAT score) and a high school grade point average of 3.50-3.74, may submit a written petition for provisional admission to the College, using a form provided by The Honors College Office upon the request of the student. (Weighted high school grade point averages certified by high schools may be used for this purpose.) A provisional admission committee consisting of the Director of The Honors College and The Honors College Office professional staff responsible for Honors advising will review the petition and determine whether provisional admission to the College should be granted. Entering freshmen who are recipients of the OSU Valedictorian Scholarship, the National Achievement Scholarship, or the National Hispanic Scholarship shall be eligible for provisional admission based on their petition and verification of their scholarship award by the Office of University Scholarships without review by the provisional admission committee.

If provisional admission is granted, it may include a limit on the number of Honors hours in which the student may enroll.

3-1-3. Transfer and Continuing Students. Transfer and continuing students who have earned at least seven (7) college credit hours will be eligible on the basis of a cumulative college grade point average which meets eligibility requirements for Honors course enrollment. [See 3-2-1.] Students other than new freshmen who do not meet the OSU and cumulative grade point average requirements because of grades earned at least two years prior to application for admission to The Honors College may petition for provisional admission on the basis of a written OSU faculty recommendation and at least one semester's academic performance at Oklahoma State University that shows to the Eligibility Appeals Committee (Section 3-2-3) that it is highly probable that the student's OSU and cumulative (not "retention") grade point averages will be at least 3.50 at the time of graduation.

3-2. ELIGIBILITY FOR CONTINUED ENROLLMENT IN HONORS COURSES

3-2-1. GRADE POINT AVERAGES REQUIRED. To be eligible for continued enrollment in Honors courses (defined as courses, sections, seminars, etc., with section numbers in the 700-range), students must maintain the following minimum OSU and cumulative (not "retention") grade point averages:

1. Fewer than 60 hours earned   3.25 (See note below.)
2. 60 - 93 hours earned   3.37
3. 94 hours earned and thereafter   3.50

Note: Freshmen failing to earn at least 2.75 OSU and cumulative grade point averages during the fall semester shall not be eligible for continued enrollment in Honors courses in the subsequent spring semester.

3-2-2. REVIEW OF RECORDS AND NOTIFICATION OF INELIGIBLE STUDENTS.

At the end of the fall semester, the Director of The Honors College shall review the academic records of all freshmen and all students granted one-semester appeal eligibility. [See 3-2-3.] In the case of freshmen who failed to achieve Oklahoma State University and cumulative grade point averages of at least 2.75 and in the case of students granted one-semester appeal eligibility who failed to achieve the cumulative grade point average required for continued enrollment in Honors courses, the Director shall notify the students by mail at their local and permanent addresses in the files of The Honors College that they are no longer eligible for Honors course enrollment and that they will be dropped from their spring semester Honors courses. The Director also shall notify the Registrar to drop these ineligible students from the class rolls for spring semester Honors sections in which they had enrolled.

At the end of the spring semester, the Director of The Honors College shall review the academic records of all students in the files of The Honors College to determine whether they meet the Oklahoma State University and cumulative grade point average criteria for continuation in the College. If it is determined that ineligible students have pre-enrolled for Honors courses for the fall semester, the Director shall notify those students by mail addressed to their local and permanent addresses on file with The Honors College that they are no longer eligible and that they must arrange to drop the Honors courses within fourteen days. If the students fail to make the schedule changes within the time period specified, the Director shall notify the Registrar to drop the ineligible students from the class rolls of the Honors courses for the fall semester.

3-2-3. APPEALS COMMITTEE FOR EXTRAORDINARY CIRCUMSTANCES. At the time students are notified of their ineligibility to continue in the Honors courses for the fall semester, they also shall be notified that if their ineligibility is the result of truly extraordinary circumstances, they may petition a faculty-student committee made up of members of the University Honors Council (with the Director not voting) and two students from the University Student Honors Council (if they are available during the summer) for an exception to the Oklahoma State University and cumulative grade point average requirement for continuation in Honors courses. The student must notify the Director of The Honors College (in writing, in person, or by telephone) of his or her intention to petition for an exception within the fourteen-day period specified in the ineligibility letter. (Upon receipt of such notification, the Director shall refrain from directing the Registrar to drop the student from Honors courses for the fall semester until the committee has reached a decision.) The student shall then transmit to the Director of The Honors College a written statement outlining his or her extenuating circumstances in time to be received within seven days from the end of the fourteen-day period specified above. The committee shall consider the petition, and a majority of those voting shall be necessary to grant an exception to the cumulative grade point requirement. The committee, at its discretion, may grant a one-semester exception or a two-semester exception to the OSU and cumulative grade point requirements for continued enrollment in Honors courses. The Director shall notify the student of the committee's decision; and, if an exception is not granted, the Director shall direct the Registrar to drop the student from class rolls of fall semester Honors courses in which the student had pre-enrolled.

3-2-4. REGAINING HONORS COLLEGE ELIGIBILITY. If a student becomes ineligible for continuation in The Honors College and later regains eligibility by improved OSU and cumulative grade point averages, the student may re-enter The Honors College and enroll in Honors courses which are available at that time. The student must provide The Honors College Office with official verification of the additional work which will restore the OSU and cumulative grade point averages to the level required for eligibility. (In the case of work appearing on the student's OSU transcript, such verification may be obtained electronically in The Honors College Office.)

3-3. REQUIREMENTS FOR GENERAL HONORS AWARD (CERTIFICATE & TRANSCRIPT ENTRY) - 21 HOURS

3-3-1. BREADTH REQUIREMENTS. Twelve hours of Honors credit (grade of "A" or "B") with a minimum of three credit hours per area from four of the following areas:

[1] English (composition and technical writing courses), Foreign Languages, Speech Communication
[2] Humanities (courses designated "H," except Foreign Languages courses)
[3] Mathematics, Statistics, Computer Science, and Management Sciences & Information Systems
[4] Natural Sciences (courses designated "N")
[5] Social Sciences (HIST 1103, JB 1393, POLS 1113, and courses designated "S," except Speech Communication)
[6] Other Courses with Honors Credit (which are not included in areas 1 through 5, above)

3-3-2. HONORS SEMINAR/INTERDISCIPLINARY HONORS COURSES. A minimum of two Honors seminars or interdisciplinary Honors courses with a minimum of four credit hours in Honors seminars or interdisciplinary Honors courses (which also may be used to satisfy a portion of the breadth requirement), grade of "A" or "B" is required.

3-3-3. ADDITIONAL HONORS HOURS. Sufficient additional hours of Honors credit (grade of "A" or "B" required) to reach total of twenty-one credit hours.

3-3-4. GRADE POINT AVERAGE. At the time of completion of the requirements for the General Honors Award, a minimum cumulative grade point average of 3.50 must have been maintained. In the case of students who have transferred hours from other institutions, a 3.50 grade point average in all hours earned at Oklahoma State University must have been maintained as well as a cumulative grade point average of 3.50 for all college work undertaken.

3-3-5. HONORS CONTRACTS. Under normal circumstances, no more than nine credit hours within the 21-hour General Honors requirement may be earned by Honors contract. In the case that scheduling conflicts make it impossible for a student to meet the 12-hour minimum in Honors sections, courses, or seminars (all designated by section numbers in the 700-range), upon recommendation of the student's academic college, the Director of The Honors College may permit an additional three hours of Honors contract credit. Honors contracts may not be utilized by transfer students to meet the minimum of six hours of Honors credit earned at Oklahoma State University for the General Honors Award. [See 3-3-6, below.]

3-3-6. TRANSFER HONORS CREDIT. In meeting the breadth requirements and Honors seminar/interdisciplinary Honors course requirements for the General Honors Award, students who have transferred from other institutions may utilize a maximum of fifteen (15) transfer Honors credit hours, including hours graded "P," "S," etc., when letter grades are not awarded in these Honors courses at the institution from which the credit has been transferred. The remaining six (6) Honors credit hours must be earned at Oklahoma State University through Honors sections or Honors seminars/interdisciplinary courses. Honors contracts may not be used for these six hours.

3-3-7. OSLEP CREDIT. With the approval of the Director of The Honors College, up to four (4) credit hours graded pass ("P") earned through the Oklahoma Scholarship-Leadership Enrichment Program (OSLEP) may be utilized toward the General Honors Award. The Director shall designate the area(s) in which such hours may be counted on a case-by-case basis.

3-3-8. CERTIFICATE AND TRANSCRIPT ENTRY. Upon the student's completion of the curricular requirements for the General Honors Award with the necessary grade point average, the Director of The Honors College shall prepare an appropriate certificate of award and notify the Registrar that the student is entitled to the "General Honors Award" transcript entry.

SECTION 4 - COLLEGE OR DEPARTMENTAL HONORS AWARD REQUIREMENTS (TRANSCRIPT ENTRY) - 12 HOURS

4-1. COLLEGE OR DEPARTMENTAL HONORS AWARD REQUIREMENTS. A college may elect to utilize a single College Honors Award or separate Departmental Honors Awards subject to college-established minimum requirements, but there shall not be a combination of a College Honors Award and Departmental Honors Awards within a single college. Criteria for admission to college/departmental Honors programs and for continuation in those programs shall be established by the academic colleges, subject to the general requirement of 3.50 OSU and cumulative grade point averages and a minimum of twelve hours of upper-division Honors credit including a creative component. In the case of students who have transferred hours from other institutions, a 3.50 grade point average in all hours earned at Oklahoma State University must have been maintained as well as a cumulative grade point average of 3.50 for all college work undertaken. [See "Top Ten Percent" alternative calculation in Section 4-4, below.]

4-2. DOUBLE MAJORS WITH HONORS AWARDS IN BOTH MAJORS. In the case of students seeking to earn a double major with Honors (any combination of Departmental and/or College Honors Awards), the student shall fulfill the requirements for both awards (including a creative component in each) and shall earn a minimum of six (6) upper-division Honors credit hours beyond the requirement for the College Honors Award or Departmental Honors Award for the student's first major. The student may count a particular course toward the Honors requirements in both majors if the course may be counted in the curricular requirements for both majors, subject to the requirement that six additional Honors hours must be earned beyond the first major's Honors requirements.

4-3. GRADE REQUIRED FOR HONORS CREDIT TOWARD AWARD. A grade of "A" or "B" shall be required in all work counting toward College or Departmental Honors Awards.

4-4. CUMULATIVE AND OSU GRADE POINT AVERAGES FOR AWARD. At the time of completion of the requirements for the College or Departmental Honors Award, a minimum 3.50 cumulative grade point average must have been maintained. In the case of students who have transferred hours from other institutions, a 3.50 grade point average in all hours earned at Oklahoma State University must have been maintained as well as a cumulative grade point average of 3.50 for all college work undertaken.

A college may, at its option, adopt a "Top Ten Percent" calculation for the College or Departmental Honors Award (for the entire college or for specified degree programs) to provide an alternative to the grade point average criteria specified in Sections 4-1 and 4-4, subject to a 3.25 OSU and cumulative grade point average minimum. Such a "Top Ten Percent" policy shall be specified in writing by the college, approved by the dean, and submitted to the Director of The Honors College. It shall be the responsibility of the college to determine which, if any, students qualify for the College or Departmental Honors Award under the alternative calculation and to notify the Director of The Honors College of the names and class rank of students meeting the criteria established by the college.

4-5. APPLICATION FOR COLLEGE OR DEPARTMENTAL HONORS AWARD. Candidates for the Departmental or College Honors Award shall file an award application form, as specified by The Honors College Office, before the beginning of their final semester or summer session. The award application form shall contain a working title for the senior Honors thesis, report, or creative component as well as the names of two faculty members who will serve as the student's committee. Prior to submission to The Honors College Office, the award application shall be approved and signed by the faculty member responsible for directing the senior Honors thesis, report, or creative component and by the Honors Director of the student's College.

4-6. DEFENSE OF CREATIVE COMPONENT. The senior Honors thesis, report, or other creative component shall be defended before a minimum of two members of the faculty who have been selected to serve as the student's committee by the Department or College.

4-7. COLLOQUIUM PRESENTATION. Candidates for the Departmental or College Honors Award shall make a public presentation of a summary of their thesis, project, or creative component in a colloquium sponsored by a Department, one of the undergraduate Colleges, or The Honors College. The method of presentation shall be that deemed appropriate for the discipline by the faculty members who serve on the student's committee. Only in circumstances in which the Dean or Honors Director of a College petitions the Director of The Honors College for a waiver of the presentation requirement may a student be excused from this requirement.

4-8. FILING OF APPROVED COPY AND ABSTRACT. Candidates for the Departmental or College Honors Award shall file one approved copy of the thesis, report, or other creative component and a one-page abstract of findings with The Honors College Office. In addition to the text, in a style and format appropriate to the discipline, the copy filed shall include an approval page, as specified by The Honors College, that shall contain the original signatures of at least two faculty members and of the Honors Director of the student's College along with the date of the successful defense of the senior Honors thesis, report, or creative component. The deadline for filing the approved copy of the thesis, report, or other creative component shall be the last day on which grades may be reported for the semester or summer session.

4-9. TRANSCRIPT ENTRY. Upon completion of the College or Departmental Honors Award, a transcript entry shall be made indicating "College Honors in [College]" or "Departmental Honors in [Department]."

5-1. GENERAL REQUIREMENTS FOR THE HONORS COLLEGE DEGREE. A student who completes a minimum of thirty-nine (39) Honors credit hours with a grade of "A" or "B" including the requirements for both the General Honors Award and for the College or Departmental Honors Award in his or her academic major with a minimum 3.50 cumulative grade point average at the time of graduation shall receive The Honors College Degree. A special Honors diploma shall be prepared, a transcript entry showing "Honors College Degree" shall be made, and the interpretative information provided by the Registrar along with transcripts shall indicate that an Honors College Degree is earned by meeting the curricular requirements of The Honors College as well as the requirements for the bachelor's degree. In the case of students who have transferred hours from other institutions, a 3.50 grade point average in all hours earned at Oklahoma State University must have been maintained as well as a cumulative grade point average of 3.50 for all college work undertaken.

5-2. GRADES REQUIRED IN HONORS WORK. A grade of "A" or "B" shall be required in all work counting toward the Honors College Degree.

5-3. TOP TEN PERCENT OPTION FOR COLLEGE. A college may, at its option, adopt a "Top Ten Percent" calculation for the Honors College Degree (for the entire college or for specified degree programs) to provide an alternative to the grade point average criteria specified above, subject to a 3.25 OSU and cumulative grade point average minimum. Such a "Top Ten Percent" policy shall be specified in writing by the college, approved by the dean, and submitted to the Director of The Honors College. It shall be the responsibility of the college to determine which, if any, students qualify for the Honors College Degree under the alternative calculation and to notify the Director of The Honors College of the names and class rank of students meeting the criteria established by the college.

5-4. HOODS FOR HONORS COLLEGE DEGREE CANDIDATES. Colleges may elect to hood candidates for The Honors College Degree at their respective convocation exercises. If they elect to do so, only those students who are candidates for The Honors College Degree shall receive the undergraduate hood. (Colleges wishing to recognize students who have earned the Departmental or College Honors Award at their convocation exercises may do so, but some form of recognition clearly distinct from the Honors hood shall be employed.) The Director of The Honors College shall transmit to the Student Union Bookstore a list of candidates for The Honors College Degree at a point near the middle of the semester.

5-5. COMMUNITY SERVICE OPTION. During the sophomore and junior years, an Honors student with OSU and cumulative grade point averages of at least 3.50 may undertake community service with an agency or organization in Stillwater or its immediate vicinity to earn waiver of one (1) to three (3) of the thirty-nine (39) Honors credit hours required for the Honors College Degree (not including any Honors hours used toward the General Honors Award or the Departmental or College Honors Award). Such community service must be undertaken while the student is enrolled on campus. A minimum of fifteen (15) hours of verified satisfactory community service shall be required for each Honors credit hour to be waived, and no more than thirty (30) hours of community service may be counted from any one semester or summer session. Community service hours shall be verified by a supervisor from the agency or organization on a form approved by the Oklahoma State University Volunteer Center or by The Honors College. With the exception of tutoring performed through University Academic Services, on-campus activities shall not be considered community service under this option. The student must certify to The Honors College that the community service hours are not being used for any course, program, requirement, or assignment on or off campus other than The Honors College's community service option under this section. Approval from the Director of The Honors College must be obtained before beginning volunteer service with an agency or organization that is not approved through the Oklahoma State University Volunteer Center. Freshmen and seniors are not eligible for this option.

5-6. INTERNATIONAL STUDY OPTION. Honors students are encouraged by The Honors College to participate in international study. An OSU Honors student with 3.50 OSU and cumulative grade point averages may earn a waiver of up to six of the six Honors credit hours required for the Honors College Degree beyond the General Honors Award and the Departmental or College Honors Award requirements.

This waiver will be awarded for college credit earned while participating in the Reciprocal Exchange Program through the OSU Study Abroad Office. One Honors hour will be waived for each three (3) semester credit hours earned (with grade of "A" or "B," or the equivalent grades in the institution attended) that count toward OSU graduation requirements. Courses completed with grades of "P," "S," etc., will be acceptable for this option when regular letter grades are not awarded in the courses at the international institution from which the credit has been transferred. The student is obligated to provide a detailed explanation of the grading system when applying for a waiver under this section.

Permission to make use of this option must be obtained in advance from the Director of The Honors College or the University Honors Council.

Students wishing to earn a waiver under this Section by participating in international study other than through the Reciprocal Exchange Program administered by the OSU Study Abroad Office must petition the Director of the Honors College or the University Honors Council in advance to do so and must demonstrate that the educational experience will be the equivalent of that offered through the Reciprocal Exchange Program in terms of classes at an international institution taught by that institution's faculty and with that institution's students.

5-7. AP and CLEP Credit Option. Students who earn credit hours by examination through the College Board's Advanced Placement Program (AP) or the College Level Examination Program (CLEP) may earn waiver of one (1) to three (3) of the thirty-nine (39) Honors credit hours required for the Honors College Degree (not including any Honors hours used toward the General Honors Award or the Departmental or College Honors Award). One Honors hour will be waived for each three (3) semester credit hours earned by AP and/or CLEP. This option applies only for courses that may be counted for credit toward the student's undergraduate degree.

SECTION 6 - HONORS COURSES

6-1. DEFINITION. An Honors course is any undergraduate course, section, seminar, tutorial, or other academic credit offering designated as such by the college in which it is offered by assignment of a section number in the 700-range. The designation of an Honors course is the prerogative and responsibility of the college granting credit.

6-2. FACULTY TEACHING HONORS SECTIONS. Only persons in tenure-track positions holding faculty rank of instructor or above, including visiting and adjunct faculty, may teach Honors courses (except in the case of Honors laboratory sections in which a separate and distinct Honors theory section is taught by a person holding faculty rank). Except in highly unusual circumstances with the advance approval of the Dean of a college and notification of the Director of The Honors College, Honors sections shall not be taught by faculty members in their first year on the faculty at Oklahoma State University. Persons holding faculty rank (instructor, lecturer, etc.) lower than assistant professor shall be permitted only for lower-division Honors courses and only if approved in advance by the dean of the undergraduate college in which the course is taught, with notification of the Director of The Honors College.

6-3. HONORS LABORATORY AND DISCUSSION SECTIONS. When the Honors component of a course is an Honors laboratory or an Honors discussion section (with Honors students having the same theory section experience as other students in the course), the Honors laboratory section or Honors discussion section must be taught by a person holding faculty rank.

6-4. CONTENT AND GRADING IN HONORS SECTIONS. Honors sections may well cover more sophisticated material than that covered in the regular sections of the same course, more active student participation should be encouraged, and the method of evaluation of students' work (examinations, reports, etc.) may be different. The grading standards at the end of the course, however, should not be designed to force the Honors students to compete among themselves for a limited number of "A" or "B" grades regardless of their level of performance. Instead, their grades should be assigned on the basis of the quality of their work-in comparison with the overall population of the course (in regular and Honors sections). In other words, the Honors student should be graded in the context of all of the students enrolled in the entire course-and not just in the context of an Honors section in isolation. Students who meet the challenge of an Honors section should have this reflected in their grades, but there should be no hesitation to award low grades to Honors students who do not live up to the expectations that are being met by other Honors students.

6-5. ENROLLMENT IN HONORS COURSES. Only undergraduate students eligible to participate in The Honors College may enroll in Honors courses (those with section numbers in the 700-range). The student's eligibility is certified to the Registrar by a trial study form stamped "Honors" by the student's academic college and also stamped "Approved" by The Honors College Office. If a student uses the drop-and-add process to add an Honors course, the drop-and-add card must be stamped "Honors" and "Approved." Simply having a copy of a trial study form stamped "Honors" and "Approved" will not allow the student to add an Honors course at a later date through the drop-and-add process without having both required stamps on the drop-and-add card.

In the case of upper-division Honors courses, if space remains after eligible undergraduate students have completed early enrollment, a dean or college Honors program director may, at his or her discretion, permit participation by graduate students along with the undergraduate students from The Honors College under the following conditions: (a) the graduate student has earned an Honors Program or Honors College Degree or maintained at least a 3.50 cumulative undergraduate grade point average, (b) the graduate student enrolls in a non-Honors section of a course number other than that of the Honors course, (c) such enrollment is approved by the Honors course faculty member on an individual basis, and (d) the total combined enrollment does not exceed the maximum originally established for the Honors course There is no right or presumption in favor of graduate student participation under the conditions specified in this section of The Honors College policies and procedures.

6-6. MAXIMUM AND MINIMUM ENROLLMENT FOR HONORS COURSES.

6-6-1. MAXIMUM ENROLLMENT. The anticipated maximum enrollment for an Honors course is twenty-two (22) students, provided however that the Director of The Honors College may, with the approval of the responsible department head, permit additional enrollment when it is likely that the normal attrition of the drop-and-add process will bring the maximum size to twenty-two students early in the semester or when requested to do so in special circumstances by the Dean of the college offering the course.

6-6-2. MINIMUM ENROLLMENT. The anticipated minimum enrollment for an Honors course is twelve (12) students in lower-division (1000- and 2000-level) and eight (8) students in upper-division (3000- and 4000-level) Honors courses and seminars. These minima are not applicable to independent study, supervised research, tutorial, or senior thesis/project courses, nor shall they preclude a department or college from offering smaller Honors courses with the approval of the dean of the college.

6-7. EVALUATION OF HONORS COURSES. All faculty members teaching Honors sections shall be encouraged to participate in the course evaluation process by distributing the University Student Honors Council's course evaluation questionnaire in their Honors sections shortly before or during pre-finals week and having the questionnaires returned to The Honors College Office. In the case of faculty teaching Honors sections funded by The Honors College, participation in the University Student Honors Council's evaluation process shall be required. Participation by faculty in the University Student Honors Council's evaluation process will be a factor taken into consideration for future funding by The Honors College.

SECTION 7 - HONORS CONTRACTS

7-1. CONTENT. Approval of the content of Honors contracts shall be obtained from the dean or Honors program director of the academic college of the faculty member responsible for the course. The Honors contract project should be one that can be completed with 20 to 25 hours of work. In the case of undergraduate students enrolled in graduate courses as part of their undergraduate program, an Honors contract indicating that the students are being graded by the same standards as graduate students in the course may be filed without requiring additional work for the Honors contract

7-2. COURSE INSTRUCTOR WITH FACULTY RANK REQUIRED. Honors contracts may be undertaken only in courses taught by persons in tenure-track positions holding faculty rank of instructor or above, including visiting and adjunct faculty. Petitions for exception to this policy may be considered by the University Honors Council and University Student Honors Council only in those cases, verified by the student's Honors advisor, in which it is not possible for the student to maintain active participant status in The Honors College by other means. In the case of courses taught by persons not holding faculty rank as specified above, if the student's petition is granted, the faculty member responsible for the course or some other faculty member designated by the department head shall be responsible for all aspects of the Honors contract and the evaluation of the contracted work.

7-3. DEADLINES. Honors contracts must be approved by the appropriate academic dean or Honors program director (Section 7-1, above) and filed by the student with the Director of The Honors College not later than the end of the third week of the semester or the end of the second week of the summer session. The Director of The Honors College may approve the late filing of an Honors contract on the recommendation of the student's academic college if the faculty member supervising the contract verifies that sufficient time remains in the semester or summer session to complete the contracted work.

7-4. GRADES IN COURSES WITH HONORS CONTRACTS. The student's grade in a course in which an Honors contract is undertaken shall not be affected by the Honors contract work. A grade of "A" or "B" must be earned in the course before Honors credit will be reflected on the student's transcript.

7-5. REPORTING. The Director of The Honors College shall be responsible for obtaining reports on completion of Honors contracts from faculty and shall submit to the Registrar a list of all students for whom Honors credit should be reflected on the students' transcripts, regardless of the college in which the faculty member is housed. The Registrar shall enter "Honors" for each course so reported.

7-6. MAXIMUM NUMBER OF CONTRACTS. Honors contracts may not be undertaken in more than two courses in a semester or summer session. The Director of The Honors College may make exceptions to this limit on the basis of a student's outstanding record in The Honors College, but no more than two Honors contracts in a semester may be counted toward the number of Honors credit hours required for active participant status in The Honors College.

7-7. HONORS CONTRACTS PERMITTED ONLY IN COURSES ACCEPTABLE FOR DEGREE CREDIT. Honors contracts are permitted only in courses that, at the time they are taken, may be counted for credit toward the student's undergraduate degree.

7-8. HONORS CONTRACT PERMISSION AFTER NOT COMPLETING HONORS CONTRACT IN EARLIER SEMESTER. Students who undertake Honors contracts are expected to complete the contracts.   When a student fails to complete an Honors contract in a course in which she earns a grade of "A" or "B," the following procedures shall apply:

After a student fails to complete the first Honors contract, the student's Honors Advisor shall contact the student concerning Honors contract expectations. The correspondence or other communication shall ask the student for a brief explanation of the reason that the contract was not completed and shall inform the student that upon receipt of such explanation, orally or in writing, additional Honors contract work may be undertaken.

After not completing a second Honors contract, the student shall be required to petition the University Honors Council and the University Student Honors Council in writing to request permission to undertake a subsequent Honors contract. Based upon the explanation contained in the written petition, the Councils (with the Honors Director not voting) shall determine whether or not the student will be permitted to undertake a subsequent Honors contract. If the Honors Councils approve the student's petition, the deadline for filing the Honors contract shall be extended to one week following approval by the Councils.

SECTION 8 - HONORS ACADEMIC ADVISING

8-1. QUALIFICATIONS FOR HONORS ADVISORS. The Director of The Honors College and the Administrative and Professional Staff of The Honors College shall provide Honors academic advising to Honors College students concerning the requirements for The Honors College awards. Honors College personnel who provide Honors academic advising shall have earned an undergraduate Honors Program or Honors College Degree.

8-2. EVALUATION OF HONORS ADVISING. Active participants in The Honors College shall be provided an opportunity to evaluate Honors advising at least once each academic year, using an evaluation form approved by the University Honors Council and University Student Honors Council.

SECTION 9 - HONORS STATUS REPORTS

The Director of The Honors College shall report to each of the academic colleges the names of their students active in The Honors College at least once a semester and, following the conclusion of the semester, shall prepare a status report on each student to be distributed to the student, the student's college, and the student's academic advisor.

SECTION 10 - PRIVILEGES EARNED BY ACTIVE PARTICIPANTS
IN THE HONORS COLLEGE

10-1. DEFINITION OF AN ACTIVE PARTICIPANT IN THE HONORS COLLEGE. An active participant in The Honors College shall be defined according to the standards set forth below:

(1) For students who have completed 0-59 credit hours (and who will not at the end of the current semester have earned the General Honors Award and six additional Honors hours including hours waived under the Community Service, International Study, and AP-CLEP Options), a minimum of six Honors hours in each semester as well as a minimum of twelve Honors hours in each two consecutive semesters shall be required to maintain active participant status. Calculation of the twelve-hour-per-two-consecutive-semesters minimum shall include the Honors hours earned (grade of "A" or "B" required) in the immediately preceding semester and the number of Honors hours in which the student is currently enrolled (in Honors courses or by Honors contracts). Summer session Honors hours shall not be included in the computation.

(2) For students who have earned (or at the end of the current semester will earn) the General Honors Award and six additional Honors hours (including hours waived under the Community Service, International Study, and AP-CLEP Options), and for students who have completed 60 or more credit hours, a minimum of three Honors hours in each semester shall be required to maintain active participant status, subject to the exceptions provided in Sections 10-1(3) and 10-1(4).

(3) Students who have earned the General Honors Award and six additional Honors hours (including hours waived under the Community Service, International Study, and AP-CLEP Options) and who continue to be eligible for Honors College participation based upon their OSU and cumulative grade point averages may be considered active participants for one subsequent semester without enrollment in Honors courses or undertaking Honors contracts by submission of a written request received by the Director of The Honors College not later than the end of the third week of classes during the fall or spring semester.

(4) Students who have completed all of The Honors College curricular requirements for the Honors College Degree but have not yet graduated (and who remain eligible for Honors College participation based upon their OSU and cumulative grade point averages) may be considered to be active participants until their graduation by submission each semester of a written request received by the Director of The Honors College not later than the end of the third week of classes during the fall or spring semester. Students who have completed all of The Honors College curricular requirements for the Honors College Degree except the senior Honors thesis or senior Honors project (and who plan to complete the senior Honors thesis or senior Honors project prior to graduation and remain eligible for Honors College participation based upon their OSU and cumulative grade point averages) also may be considered to be active participants by filing the same form of written request.

(5) Part-time students (defined as students enrolled for fewer than twelve credit hours in either the fall or spring semester), upon their request, shall be considered active in The Honors College if the number of Honors hours successfully completed in the immediately preceding semester and the number of Honors hours in which the student is currently enrolled (in Honors sections or by Honors contracts) is equal to the proportion of Honors hours normally required of a full-time student enrolled in twelve hours per semester under subsections (1) and (2), above.

(6) Students participating in the International Study Option of The Honors College (Section 5-6, above) who are enrolled in at least as many credit hours at the international institution as would be required by Oklahoma State University to be considered a full-time student for the current academic semester shall be considered active in The Honors College.

10-2. EARLY ENROLLMENT. The Director of The Honors College shall report to the Registrar, through appropriate channels, the names and student identification numbers of those students who meet the definition of an active Honors College student (Section 10-1, above) during a given semester and, therefore, qualify for early enrollment for the next academic semester and/or summer session.

Active Honors College students will be permitted to begin early enrollment at 8:00 a.m. on the date specified by the Registrar.

10-3. HONORS COLLEGE STUDY LOUNGE. Active participants in The Honors College are entitled to use The Honors College Study Lounge in the Edmon Low Library.

10-4. EXTENDED LIBRARY CHECK-OUT PRIVILEGES. Active participants in The Honors College are entitled to check out materials from the Library on the same basis as graduate students.

10-5. ACTIVE PARTICIPANT STATUS - EXCEPTIONS UNDER EXTRAORDINARY CIRCUM-STANCES. In the event of extraordinary circumstances that prevent a student from undertaking the necessary number of Honors credit hours for active participant status in a given semester, a student may submit a written petition to the Director of The Honors College to be considered an active participant in The Honors College.

The petition process under this section may not be used by students who have failed to earn the OSU and cumulative grade point averages required for eligibility in The Honors College.

Approval for such petitions shall be limited to unusual circumstances in which no reasonable alternative exists for the student.

Such petition may be approved by the Director of The Honors College or referred at the student's request to the University Honors Council and University Student Honors Council for a decision on the basis of the student's petition and record of performance in The Honors College.

LEARNING OUTCOMES ASSESSMENT
NORTHERN ARIZONA UNIVERSITY

READING ASSESSMENT GOALS for HON 190/191

The following is a list of reading skills that we expect our Honors freshmen students to master in Honors 190/191.

Contextual Analysis

1. Students will be able to critique a work of fiction or non-fiction with respect to its genre, themes, issues, style, point of view, characterization, setting, plot, imagery, rhetorical strategies, prosodic techniques, and so on.
2. Students will be able to compare and contrast two written works with respect to their genres, styles, ideas, theses, settings, cultural contexts, and so on.
3. Students will be able to identify and critically assess a particular text's audience.
4. Students will be able to critique a piece of writing with respect to ethos, pathos, and logos.
5. Students will be able to critique and contextualize their readings from a cultural, historical, sociological, psychological, scientific, religious, ethnic, and/or philosophical point of view.
6. Students will be able to examine a text and argue persuasively the merits of a text with respect to certain assumptions, key concepts and ideas, claims, and supporting evidence.

Applied Skills

7. Students will be able to summarize, orally or in written form, the plot of a work of fiction or non-fiction (e.g., novel, short story, autobiographical essay, etc).
8. Students will be able to paraphrase, orally or in written form, a poem.
9. Students will be able to identify and summarize, orally or in written form, the thesis and main points of a secondary source (e.g., chapter in book of critical essays, journal article, newspaper article, refereed on-line web source, etc.).
10. Students will be able to create a well-organized and hierarchical outline of ideas, main points, and/or issues based upon their reading of a particular text.

APPENDIX H

HONORS ADVISING SURVEYS

H-1. HONORS COLLEGE ADVISING SURVEY - KENT STATE UNIVERSITY

YOU ARE IMPORTANT TO US. We will use your feedback to evaluate the strengths and limitations of our advising program. We will seriously consider your suggestions. Please complete this form and turn it in at the front desk, then **enter your name in the Advising Survey Drawing!**

My advisor is (circle): Andrews, Bocchicchio, Craig, Crawford, Gares, Sampson, Sharma

My class is (circle): Freshman Sophomore Junior Senior

I have declared a major (circle): Yes No

How many times have you seen your Honors advisor since school started this year? _________

Use this scale to rate the items in the two sections below:
1 - Strongly Disagree 2 - Disagree 3 - Neutral 4 - Agree 5 - Strongly Agree

Please **rate yourself as an advisee.**

1.	I make an effort to know my advisor and to help my advisor know me.	1 2 3 4 5
2.	I make and keep appointments with my advisor. I call to cancel an appointment if I can't make it.	1 2 3 4 5
3.	I strive to clarify my personal values and goals in advance of advising appointments.	1 2 3 4 5
4.	I read the catalog and requirement sheet to try to understand my liberal education requirements and program requirements.	1 2 3 4 5
5.	I prepare a possible class schedule and options/questions BEFORE my advising appointment	1 2 3 4 5
6.	I accept responsibility for my own academic progress.	1 2 3 4 5

Please **rate your Honors College advisor.**

7.	My advisor is adequately available during regular office hours.	1 2 3 4 5
8.	My advisor responds promptly to my telephone and e-mail questions.	1 2 3 4 5
9.	My advisor takes time to become personally acquainted with me.	1 2 3 4 5
10.	My advisor is someone with whom I can talk freely.	1 2 3 4 5
11.	My advisor is a careful listener and checks to make sure we have understood each other.	1 2 3 4 5
12.	My advisor provides me with information I need about the catalog.	1 2 3 4 5
13.	My advisor is able to refer me to persons or offices within the university where I can get answers to questions.	1 2 3 4 5
14.	My advisor is knowledgeable about Honors requirements.	1 2 3 4 5
15.	My advisor encourages me to get involved with campus activities.	1 2 3 4 5
16.	My advisor suggests ways I can explore different majors.	1 2 3 4 5
17.	My advisor has discussed my long-range life and career goals with me.	1 2 3 4 5
18.	My advisor has discussed my academic goals and progress with me.	1 2 3 4 5
19.	My advisor expects me to be a responsible partner in the advising process.	1 2 3 4 5
20.	My advisor encourages me to make my own decisions.	1 2 3 4 5

Comments/Suggestions/Advice for your advisor:

H-2. HONORS ADVISING QUESTIONNAIRE - OKLAHOMA STATE UNIVERSITY

Please take a few minutes to complete this questionnaire and bring it with you to your Honors advising appointment so that you can drop it in the box in The Honors College Office. Thank you.

1. Your Honors advisor (please circle):   Campbell   Dillin   Roark   Spurrier

2. How long has this person been your Honors advisor?

3. Your college (please circle):   AG   AS   BU   ED   EN   HE   UAS

4. Your classification (please circle):   Freshman   Sophomore   Junior   Senior

5. Approximately how many times have you seen your Honors advisor this school year?

    Was this a sufficient number of times? (please circle)   Yes   No

    If "no," please explain briefly.

6. At this point, do you plan to complete your Honors College Degree?   Yes   No   Unsure
    How would you describe your experience with your Honors advisor?

Please indicate your responses on items 8-12 dealing with your Honors advisor, using "4" as the best score and "0" as the worst score. "N/A" means that this item is not applicable to you.

8. Knowledge and explanation of Honors College policies   4   3   2   1   N/A

9. Assistance in planning your Honors class schedule to meet
    Honors College award requirements   4   3   2   1   N/A

10. Ability to refer you to other services on campus (if requested)   4   3   2   1   N/A

11. Availability to answer your questions   4   3   2   1   N/A

12. Cares about you as a person   4   3   2   1   N/A
     Please feel free to comment on any of these items.

13. What advice would you give your Honors advisor?

14. How would you describe your regular academic advisor's attitude toward your participation
     in The Honors College? (please circle)

            Supportive   Neutral   Not Supportive

HONORS STUDENT SURVEYS

I-1. HONORS STUDENT SURVEY - UNIVERSITY OF NORTHERN COLORADO

What is your current status on campus? Please circle one.

freshman   sophomore   junior   senior

When did you join the University Honors Program? Please circle one.

freshman   sophomore   junior   senior

What is your major? ____

What most interested you in the Honors Program at UNC? Check all that apply.
____ Extra academic challenge
____ Faculty involved with Honors and Life of the Mind
____ Honors as a possible way to strengthen my career and/or graduate school opportunities
____ Honors Connections Seminars (Hon 100/200 classes)
____ Involvement of Honors in campus activities, such as Academic Excellence Week and the International Film Series
____ Life of the Mind courses (MIND designated classes)
____ Opportunity to do a thesis
____ Prestige and recognition promised
____ Scholarship opportunities
____ Students already in Honors
____ Student Honors Council and its activities
____ A specific person (please specify) ____
____ Other (please specify) ____

Of the choices given below, please rank the top 10 STRENGTHS in the University Honors Program administration, with 1 being the largest strength.
____ Advising
____ E-mail news and updates
____ Enrichment provided in your major through the Honors experience
____ Faculty involved with Honors and Life of the Mind
____ Honors Connections Seminars (Hon 100/200 classes)
____ Honors Handbook
____ Honors Newsletter
____ Honors Research/Thesis courses (Hon 351 and 451 classes)
____ Intellectual challenge
____ Involvement of Honors in campus activities, such as Academic Excellence Week and the International Film Series
____ Life of the Mind courses (MIND designated classes)
____ Personal attention from faculty
____ Recognition that you receive
____ Relationships you establish with other Honors students and faculty
____ Research Day
____ Scholarship opportunities
____ Student Honors Council and its activities
____ Website
____ Works in Progress Symposium
____ Other (please specify) ____

Of the choices given below, please rank the top 5 WEAKNESSES in the University Honors Program administration, with 1 being the largest weakness:

____Advising
____E-mail news and updates
____Enrichment provided in your major through the Honors experience
____Faculty involved with Honors and Life of the Mind
____Honors Connections Seminars (Hon 100/200 classes)
____Honors Handbook
____Honors Newsletter
____Honors Research/Thesis courses (Hon 351 and 451 classes)
____Intellectual challenge
____Involvement of Honors in campus activities, such as Academic Excellence Week and the International Film Series
____Life of the Mind courses (MIND designated classes)
____Personal attention from faculty
____Recognition that you receive
____Relationships you establish with other Honors students and faculty
____Research Day
____Scholarship opportunities
____Student Honors Council and its activities
____Website
____Works in Progress Symposium
____Other (please specify) ____

What have been the most important Student Honors Council activities for you? Check all that apply.

____Community Service Projects
____Fall Retreat
____General Meetings
____Honors Newsletter
____International Film Series
____Intramural Sports
____New Student Workshop
____Peer Advising
____Pizza Seminars
____Other (please specify) ____

Overall, how would you rate your University Honors Program experience?

1= Excellent 5= Poor

Academically	1	2	3	4	5
In Advising	1	2	3	4	5
Socially	1	2	3	4	5

Thank you!

Please return this survey to the University Honors Program office in Michener L-95 or mail it to Campus Box 13, Greeley, CO 80639 by October 31.

I-2. WESTMINSTER COLLEGE HONORS PROGRAM
GRADUATING SENIOR EXIT SURVEY

This survey helps us obtain information about your Honors program experience. Your responses are very important because they will allow us to evaluate the strengths and limitations of the program and to make appropriate changes. Please complete this form as thoroughly as possible and return it by June 1, either in electronic format or as a hard copy. We really appreciate your thoughtful responses. Thank you.

NAME: ____

STUDENT ID#: ____

MAJOR(s): ____

MINOR(s): ____

GRADUATION DATE: ____

GRADUATING WITH (check one):   [ ] Honors Degree   [ ] Honors Certificate

TITLE OF THESIS (for Honors Degree Students):

POSITIONS OF LEADERSHIP IN WESTMINSTER COLLEGE'S HONORS PROGRAM (i.e., Student Honors Council, Honors Peer Mentor, Honors Newsletter editor, Honors START Center Advisor, etc.):

OTHER HONORS ACHIEVEMENT (identify/explain any that apply):

1. Honors Writing Awards (year/title/category):

2. Participation in Honors regional/national conference (year/nature of participation):

3. Independent Summer Research Grant (year/title of grant):

4. Published in *Scribendi*, the journal of the Western Regional Collegiate Honors Council:

5. Other: ____

What are your plans after graduating from Westminster (pick one that best applies)?

1. Name of Graduate/Professional School: ________________________________

   Degree Sought: ____

   Scholarships/Fellowships: ____

2. Name of Employer and Title: ____

3. Uncertain. I am considering: _______________________________________

Five years from now, what do you hope to be doing?

NARRATIVE RESPONSES (please be as specific as possible)

1. From your experience, identify the most positive features of the Honors Program in its current configuration.

2. From your experience, identify any negative features. What recommendations would you have for strengthening the program?

3. What was the best Honors course you took? What was it that made it the "best"?

4. What was the weakest Honors course you took? Explain why.

5. How were your Honors courses different from your non-Honors courses?

6. Did you find your Honors courses challenging? In what ways?

7. Was the Honors program successful in giving you a sense of community? How could that community be strengthened?

8. How has the program changed over the years you have been here?

9. What other additions and/or changes would you make to the Honors program?

10. Are you glad you participated in the Honors program? Why or why not?

11. Identify the specific skills that the Honors program has helped you cultivate, either through its curriculum or related programs.

PROGRAM ACTIVITIES (please identify the following Honors-related activities that you participated in)

	Once	A Few Times	Regularly	Always
1. Pizza with Profs	[ ]	[ ]	[ ]	[ ]
2. Profs Pick the Flick	[ ]	[ ]	[ ]	[ ]
3. Reading Honorable Mention	[ ]	[ ]	[ ]	[ ]
4. Annual Spring Honors Banquet	[ ]	[ ]	[ ]	[ ]
5. Annual Honors Writing Award Competition	[ ]	[ ]	[ ]	[ ]
6. Honors Resource Library	[ ]	[ ]	[ ]	[ ]
7. Sending a Message to the Honors Listserv	[ ]	[ ]	[ ]	[ ]

HONORS PROGRAM MISSION

The Honors program is guided by a mission statement designed by the Honors Council. Please
consider the following features of the Honors mission and think about how the Honors program
(curriculum and other resources) helped advance these aims. Check the box that applies.

	Strongly Agree	Agree	Neutral	Disagree	Strongly Disagree
1. I developed confidence in my ability to understand and discuss complex ideas and texts.	[ ]	[ ]	[ ]	[ ]	[ ]
2. I developed confidence in my ability to engage in problem solving and research design.	[ ]	[ ]	[ ]	[ ]	[ ]
3. I strengthened my written and oral communication skills.	[ ]	[ ]	[ ]	[ ]	[ ]
4. I mastered an ability to work effectively in groups of diverse people.	[ ]	[ ]	[ ]	[ ]	[ ]
5. I made connections between disciplines.	[ ]	[ ]	[ ]	[ ]	[ ]
6. I learned to apply new knowledge and skills in meaningful ways that will help me succeed in my professional and personal life following college.	[ ]	[ ]	[ ]	[ ]	[ ]
7. I had access to a range of supplemental experiences of an academic and social nature with similarly motivated and talented students.	[ ]	[ ]	[ ]	[ ]	[ ]

SUMMARY COMMENTS

We believe that the best and most accurate representatives of the Honors program are the students who participate in Honors. Please use this space to make any final, summary comments
about your experience in Westminster College's Honors program. (Would you be willing to allow
us to reproduce any of the comments below in publicity materials used in recruiting students-i.e.,
Honors website, brochures, etc.?   Yes [ ]   No [ ])

The following survey is for the benefit of the University Honors Program. No names should appear on this form. *When completed, detach this page from the packet and return it separately to the UHP office.*

Rate the following: A = Excellent
                       B = Good
                       C = Fair
                       D = Poor

General Education (breadth of knowledge) received at UNM	A	B	C	D
In-depth Education in your Major Field	A	B	C	D
Education in the Honors Program	A	B	C	D
Instructors in the Honors Program	A	B	C	D
The UHP Legacy Seminars	A	B	C	D
UHP Senior Colloquium	A	B	C	D
UHP Seminar Content (in general)	A	B	C	D
The Texts and Materials Used in Seminars	A	B	C	D
Extra-Curricular and other out-of-class Honors activities	A	B	C	D
Sense of Community in Honors Center	A	B	C	D
The Honors Office Staff	A	B	C	D
UHP Seminars helped improve ability to write effectively.	A	B	C	D
UHP Seminars helped improve ability to think critically.	A	B	C	D
UHP Seminars helped improve ability to speak effectively.	A	B	C	D
UHP Seminars helped improve ability to learn independently.	A	B	C	D
UHP Seminars helped improve research skills.	A	B	C	D

Comments:

What do you view as the major strength(s) of your education at UNM? (include outstanding courses/faculty and/or extracurricular activities)

What do you view as the major strength of your UHP experience?

What do you view as the major weakness of your education at UNM?

What do you view as the major weakness of your UHP experience?

Would you recommend the Honors Program to other qualified students?   Yes   No
Explain.

APPENDIX J. GRADUATION CHECKLIST - UNIVERSITY OF NEW MEXICO

UHP Graduation Packet Checklist
Please read very carefully and **retain this page** for future reference!
This exit process is for students graduating this semester only.

Graduation Packet due March 11th!

1. _____ **REVIEW STUDENT FILE**
Please review your personal folder in the Honors office. You may add to your file any additional documentation that you feel reflects your academic, social and community service experience as an undergraduate.

2. _____ **SENIOR REVIEW FORM**
Complete the "Senior Review" form and return with your complete packet. Please write legibly or type!

3. _____ **UHP COURSEWORK FORM**
Complete the "UHP Coursework Summary" form and return with your complete packet. Please write legibly or type!

4. _____ **UNM TRANSCRIPTS**
Submit an unofficial copy of your UNM transcript(s) with your complete packet.

5. _____ **TRANSFER TRANSCRIPTS**
If you are a transfer student, submit an unofficial copy of your transfer transcript(s) with your complete packet.

6. _____ **SEMINAR PAPER**
Include one written paper (essay, research, creative prose) from an Honors seminar with your complete packet.

7. _____ **SENIOR SURVEY FORM**
Complete the "Senior Survey" form and return with your complete packet. Please write legibly or type!

8. _____ **HONORS CERTIFICATE AND ACCOMMODATION REQUESTS FORM**
Complete the "Honors Certificate" form indicating how you would like your name to appear on your Honors Certificate and indicate any needs for the graduation ceremony. Return the form with your complete packet.

9. _____ **PHOTOGRAPH**

> *Ask one of the Honors office staff to take a Polaroid of you. The picture will be placed in your student file for future reference (our memories aren't reliable).*

10. _____ **EXIT INTERVIEW**
After the senior packet deadline, the UHP office will send a letter to you telling with whom you'll interview and where to contact him/her. You ARE REQUIRED to have a 30-minute exit interview with a member of the University Honors Council or the UHP Director. YOU are responsible for arranging an appointment for your exit interview. Interviews must be completed before the final Honors Council meeting.

11. ____ **RECOGNITION CEREMONY**

Information regarding your Honors designation and the Honors Senior Recognition Ceremony, as well as complimentary invitations, will be mailed to you approximately two weeks prior to the ceremony. Attendance is expected of all seniors at the Recognition Ceremony. **Dress for the ceremony is semi-formal. (No Cap & Gown required.)**

Determining Levels of Honors for Seniors

Range of GPA:

3.20 - 3.49	*Cum Laude*
3.50 - 3.89	*Magna Cum Laude*
3.90 - 4.00	*Summa Cum Laude*

The Honors Council clearly does not rigidly apply set GPA cutoffs, but instead exercises flexibility in considering individual cases on their own merit. In recent years, the Council has also avoided setting any rigid quotas on the number of *summas* or *magnas*.

Besides GPA, the following other criteria have emerged by consensus as the most important in considering the levels of Honors:

1. Breadth: How widely has the student sampled coursework in the major areas of knowledge including the humanities, social sciences, math and science, the arts? Has the student been able to fashion a program that gives him or her the semblance of being "educated?" If in a restrictive pre-professional school, how widely has the student used Honors seminars to sample areas of knowledge beyond his or her narrow specialization?

2. Difficulty: Has the student elected a course of study that has been challenging? Are a disproportionate number of seminars at the 200 level? If the student is in a department with a strong departmental Honors program, has he or she taken advantage of it?

3. Honors Seminars: Has the student taken a broad range of seminars from various professors vs. seminars from the same professor? Do the evaluations from the UHP faculty indicate engagement in the seminars, solid Honors level work? Does the student have the requisite number of courses? Has the student participated in cross-cultural/multicultural experiences or courses at UNM?

4. Extracurricular Involvement: To what degree has the student been engaged in activities within the university, the community, or the UHP that contribute something back to the general sense of community?

5. Abilities: Has the student demonstrated knowledge, skills, and ability in writing, critical/creative thinking, and articulate oral expression (based on the essay submitted and faculty comments)?

6. Work: Has the student by necessity or for professional reasons devoted hours to outside employment, which may have affected any of the areas above?

7. Advance Placement: If a student entered UNM with advanced credits, how did he or she utilize the extra freedom to choose coursework?

8. Other Extenuating Circumstances: Health, family responsibilities, returning student status, academic renewal, transfer status–all have been considered in individual cases in the past.

UHP SENIOR REVIEW FORM

The following information will be considered by the University Honors Council to determine your level of Honors. Council members read Senior Review responses carefully. This form will be placed in your Honors Student file and treated as confidential. **(Please type or legibly print all information.)**

Name: ____
First   Middle   Last

Social Security #: _____________________________ Local phone Number: _______________

E-mail address: ____

Local Address: ____
Street/Apt., City, State, Zip Code

Permanent Address: ____
Street/Apt., City, State, Zip Code

High School Attended: ____
Name   Year Graduated

____
City, State

Are you a Transfer Student?   Yes   No

If yes: School: _____________________________ Total Transfer Credits: ____________
Name

____
City, State

What UNM College are you graduating from?

College: ____

Major(s) ____________________________ Minor(s) _____________________________

Current Cumulative GPA: __________________ Total Credit Hours at Graduation: _________

Have you received any Scholarships?   Yes   No

If yes: Which scholarships?

        __ Regents   __ Presidential   ___ Amigo   __ Excel

        __ UHP Stipend   __ Lottery Success   ___ NM Scholars

        __ Other:____

Have you received any educational loans?   Yes   No

Have you been employed during your college career?   Yes   No

If yes: For how many years: On campus:____ Off campus: ___ Average Hrs Per Week: ___

Campus Activities (Indicate your role/any offices held.):

H.S.A.C. _______________________________ *Scribendi* _______________________

ASUNM _________________________________ Fraternity/Sorority _______________

Resident Halls Government ________________ Sports ___________________________

Daily Lobo ______________________________ Performing Arts __________________

Clubs/Organizations ____

Other ____

Honors and Awards:
___ Phi Eta Sigma   ___ Sigma Tau Delta   __ Order of Omega   __ Golden Key
___ Phi Beta Kappa   ___ Phi Kappa Phi   Other: ______________________________

Fellowship(s): ____

Publications/Presentations (Titles, Dates, etc.):

Scribendi ____

Conceptions Southwest ____

Best Student Essays ____

WRHC Conference ____

NCHC Conference ____

Other ____

Other Activities (National/International Studies, Co-op Education, Research, Internships, etc.):

____

____

____

____

____

Cross-cultural & Multi-cultural Experiences (List specific programs and courses, such as Conexiones, study abroad, languages, etc.):

____

____

____

____

Plans for the Next Year (Graduate School, Professional School, etc.):

____

____

____

____

Professional Plans for the Future:

____

____

____

____

UHP COURSEWORK SUMMARY

NAME:_________________________________ SS#: _______________________________

I. UHP REQUIRED SEMINARS - one at each level.

SEMINAR TITLE	GRADE & YR	SEMINAR INSTRUCTOR
100 Level		
200 Level		
300 Level		
400 Level		

Senior Options:

Colloquium ____

Service Learning Project ____

UHP Thesis Title ____

Student Teaching (Course/Co-Teacher) ____________________________________

Department Honors Thesis/Project ____

    Department _________________________________ Director _____________________________

II. UHP ELECTIVES - 6 credit hours for minimum 21 hours necessary to graduate with University Honors and additional seminars completed (If graduating under 2003 catalog, 24 total hours are necessary).

LEVEL	SEMINAR TITLE	GRADE & YR	SEMINAR INSTRUCTOR
_______	_______________	___________	_________________
_______	_______________	___________	_________________
_______	_______________	___________	_________________
_______	_______________	___________	_________________

III. WAIVED SEMINAR (requires prior approval by Director)

LEVEL	SEMINAR TITLE	GRADE & YR	SEMINAR INSTRUCTOR
_______	_______________	___________	_________________

IV. TRANSFER HONORS COURSES

LEVEL	SEMINAR TITLE	GRADE & YR	SEMINAR INSTRUCTOR
_______	_______________	___________	_________________
_______	_______________	___________	_________________
_______	_______________	___________	_________________

To give the Council a sense of your overall undergraduate course distribution, indicate the number of credit hours completed in the following categories. Assign interdisciplinary courses such as Honors program, Women Studies, etc., to the most appropriate category possible:

COMMUNICATION:

English Writing _____________

Commun/Journ _____________

Linguistics ________________

HUMANITIES:

Literature ____________

History ____________

Phil/Religion _________

BIOL/BEHAV. SCIENCES:

Anthropology___________

Biology ______________

Psychology ___________

PHYSICAL SCIENCES:

Astronomy _______________

Chemistry ______________

Geology_______________

Physics ______________

SOCIAL SCIENCES:

Anthropology _________

Economics _________

Geography _________

Political Sci _________

Sociology___________

FINE ARTS:

Art History ____________

Dance ______________

Film ________________

Music______________

Theater Arts ___________

OTHERS:

Mathematics _________________   Pharmacy ____________   Management___________

Education ___________________   Architecture__________   Engineering

Nursing ____________________   Foreign Language______

Other (List): ____

OPTIONAL: The following information provides data for UNM statistical information.

Ethnicity: Anglo   African American   Native American   Hispanic   Asian   Other

Age: 18-22   23-27   28-32   33-37   38-45   46 & Over

Marital Status: Single   Divorced   Married   Widowed

Sex: Male   Female

K-1. ALUMNI QUESTIONNAIRE - ABLIENE CHRISTIAN UNIVERSITY

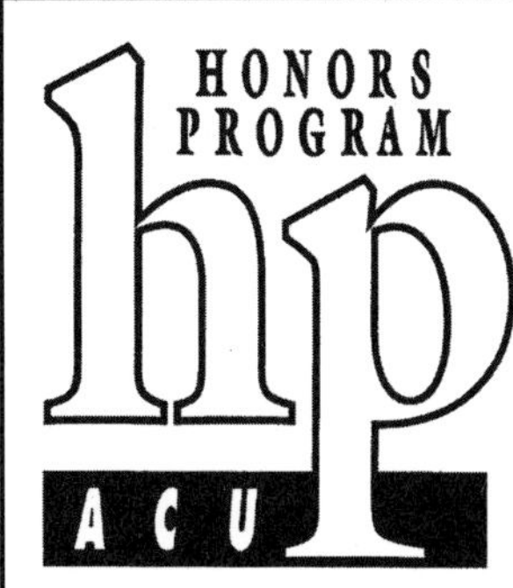

Abilene Christian University Honors Program
Survey of Alumni Attitudes - Fall 2002

Please answer the following questions by either circling the correct response or by providing the requested information. Giving your name is optional. Your answers will be held in strict confidence, and you will not be identified with your responses. Your cooperation is important to us as we gather information on student and alumni perceptions of the Honors Program. We enclose a business-reply envelope for your convenience.

Dear Honors Exes:
We're asking for your help in our Program Review for the University. Please return this survey by the end of November. The advice you give us will help in improving curriculum and benefits. The HP is 18 years old and still having fun, challenging ACU's brightest students. We appreciate your help.

Dr. W.

1. What is your gender?
    a. Male
    b. Female

2. What is your age? _______ Years

3. What is your race?
    a. Black   c. White   e. Other
    b. Asian   d. Hispanic

4. What is your marital status?
    a. Never married   c. Widowed   e. Separated
    b. Divorced   d. Married

5. In what state do you live? _________________

6. What is the size of your community?
    a. Rural or farm area
    b. Small town or city (under 50,000)
    c. Medium city/metro area (50,000 to 250,000)
    d. Large city/metro area (over 250,000)

7. What is your current employment status? (Circle all that apply.)
    a. Employed full-time
    b. Employed part-time
    c. Unemployed, seeking employment (go to question 11)
    d. Homemaker (go to question 11)
    e. Full-time student (go to question 11) where _______________
    f. Part-time student (go to question 11) where _______________

8. Are you currently employed in an occupation related to your major field of study?
    a. Yes
    b. No

9. What is your occupation? (Please be specific and include your job title.)

    ____

    ____

    ____

10. Last year, what was your income before taxes, excluding any income earned by other
    members of your family?
    a. Under $10,000   e. $40,000 to $49,999   i. $80,000 to $89,999
    b. $10,000 to $19,999   f. $50,000 to $59,999   j. $90,000 to $99,999
    c. $20,000 to $29,999   g. $60,000 to $69,999   k. Over $100,000
    d. $30,000 to $39,999   h. $70,000 to $79,999

11. If you received a Bachelor's degree from ACU, please give the degree(s), major(s), and
    date.

    ____

    ____

12. Did you complete the Honors Program requirements?
    __ Yes. University Honors (30 hrs)
    __ Yes. Department Honors (12 hrs)

13. If you received your Bachelor's degree from another institution, please indicate the insti-
    tution, date, and field:

    ____

14. Did you receive a Master's degree from ACU?
    a. Yes   Please provide date and field.

    ____

    b. No

15. What is the highest degree you have received from any institution?
    a. Bachelor's   b. Master's   c. Doctorate (Ph.D., J.D., M.D., O.D., etc.)
    Please indicate the institution, degree, date, and field if different from questions 13 or 14.

    ____

16. Did you participate in any departmental activities while at ACU?
    ____ Band/Choir   ____ Missions trips   ____ Sports
    ____ Social club   ____ Volunteer work   ____ Publications
    ____ Musical   ____ Student Association   ____ Other
    ____ Sing Song   ____ Local Church Work
    ____ Theater   ____ Dept. Organization

For each of the following questions circle your answer by using the following codes:
5= strongly agree, 4= agree, 3= undecided, 2= disagree, 1= strongly disagree.

17. Regarding my Honors Program work at ACU, I am satisfied with the

	SA	A	U	D	SD	N/A
a. Overall quality of the Honors Program	5	4	3	2	1	0
b. Quality of instruction in lower-level and colloquia courses	5	4	3	2	1	0
c. Quality of instruction in upper-level contracts and projects	5	4	3	2	1	0
d. Opportunities for interaction with the HP teachers (including director of contracts or projects)	5	4	3	2	1	0
e. Professional competence of the HP teachers	5	4	3	2	1	0
f. Quality of the HP courses in preparing me for employment	5	4	3	2	1	0
g. Quality of HP courses, contracts, or independent study in preparing me for graduate or professional school	5	4	3	2	1	0
h. Range of subjects available in HP courses including colloquia	5	4	3	2	1	0
i. Availability of my Honors advisor to meet with me	5	4	3	2	1	0
j. Range of options for meeting HP requirements	5	4	3	2	1	0
k. Depth of engagement with subject matter in HP classes and projects	5	4	3	2	1	0
l. Challenge presented by the HP work	5	4	3	2	1	0
m. Fairness of grading in my HP courses	5	4	3	2	1	0
n. Availability of co-curricular activities for HP students (fall picnic, etc.)	5	4	3	2	1	0
o. Practicum or internship experience for HP credit	5	4	3	2	1	0
p. Classroom facilities related to the HP and equipment used in HP work	5	4	3	2	1	0
q. Clarity of HP requirements	5	4	3	2	1	0
r. Opportunities for student participation in HP decisions	5	4	3	2	1	0
s. Influence of the HP on the ACU academic climate	5	4	3	2	1	0
t. Opportunities for student evaluation of instruction in HP classes	5	4	3	2	1	0
u. My decision to finish or not to finish HP requirements	5	4	3	2	1	0

18. At this point in my career, I am satisfied with

	SA	A	U	D	SD	N/A
a. The level of my responsibilities	5	4	3	2	1	0
b. The type of work I am doing	5	4	3	2	1	0
c. My income	5	4	3	2	1	0
d. The field in which I am working	5	4	3	2	1	0
e. My prospects for advancement	5	4	3	2	1	0
f. My opportunities for professional development	5	4	3	2	1	0

19. Based on your career experience thus far, what else do you wish the HP had done to enhance your professional and personal life?

20. Was the HP work worth your time? Please explain.

21. Did the HP work help you get into graduate studies or get a job? If so, how?

22. Based on your career experience thus far, what single change would you make within the HP if given the opportunity?

23. The Honors Program is currently considering the option of offering 3 separate ways to graduate with Honors Program distinction: 18 hours of freshman/sophomore work = Honors Associate; 12 hours of junior/senior level work (3 hours of colloquia, two upper-level contracts, and a capstone project) = Departmental Honors; all of the above = University Honors. What do you think about having these three ways to graduate with Honors distinction? Should there be any more?

24. Assessment of Honors developmental goals:

	SA	A	U	D	SD	N/A
My experience in the Honors Program at ACU has helped me to think more integratively and critically	5	4	3	2	1	0
My experience in the Honors Program at ACU has helped me become more globally aware	5	4	3	2	1	0
My experience in the Honors Program at ACU has helped me be able to present the results of critical reflection in a coherent and professional manner	5	4	3	2	1	0
My experience in the Honors Program at ACU has helped me be more markedly competent in at least one academic or professional field	5	4	3	2	1	0

25. Do you have any other comments or information that might be helpful to us? If so, please put them below.

Please return this information in the enclosed pre-paid envelope. There is no need to put your name on this form. Thank you so much for making our Honors Program better!

HONORS COLLEGE ALUMNI SURVEY
Kent State University

Name ____
      (First)   (Initial)   (Maiden)   (Last)

Street Address ____

City/State/Zip ____

Day Phone ______________________________ **Evening Phone** ___________________________

E-mail Address ____

Year Graduated ________________ **Undergraduate Major** ______________________________

Ethnic Heritage: African American ____ White/non-Hispanic _____ Hispanic _____ Asian ____

Native American ______ Other ________________________________

Gender: Female ______ Male ______

Where did you begin your undergraduate studies?

Kent Campus ________ Regional Campus ________ Other ________

How many years were you in Honors? ____

What is your current occupational status? (Check all that apply.)

_____ working full time _____ in school: full time ____ part time ____

_____ working part time: one __ two ___ three+ jobs_____ _____ homemaker, caretaker

_____ unemployed, laid-off, looking for work _____ retired

Who is your current employer? ____

What is your present job title? ____

What is your annual salary or wage (including commissions, etc.) in your current position?

______ less than $20,000 ______ $60,000-$79,999

______ $20,000-$39,999 ______ $80,000-$99,999

______ $40,000-$59,999 ______ $100,000 and over

Have you reoriented career goals since graduation? Yes ________ No _________

If so, why? ____

List the titles of your last three jobs. _______________________________________

____

List any post-baccalaureate studies you have undertaken/are undertaking.

<u>Date</u>   <u>Institution</u>   <u>Major</u>   <u>Degree</u>

List a few of your graduate-level and/or career awards and Honors if applicable.

In what ways, if any, was your Honors education good preparation for graduate school, work, or other aspects of your personal life?

Were you awarded a scholarship from Honors? Yes _______ No _____

If yes, did that scholarship make a difference in your decision to choose to attend Kent State?

       Yes _______ No _______

Was being a part of Honors a factor in your decision to attend Kent State?

       Yes _______ No _______

Based on your perceptions, please answer the following questions by circling the appropriate number to indicate your response on this scale:

        (1) strongly agree (2) agree (3) disagree (4) strongly disagree.

My Honors experience:

a. had a significant positive effect on my educational   1   2   3   4
     development and creativity.

b. contributed significantly to my personal enrichment.   1   2   3   4

c. provided me with intellectual challenge.   1   2   3   4

d. was satisfactorily assisted and guided by my Honors advisor.   1   2   3   4

e. prepared me for my future educational and career goals.   1   2   3   4

f.   provided me with closer interaction with faculty and other   1   2   3   4
     Honors students.

g.   increased my awareness and appreciation of the arts.   1   2   3   4

h.   increased my awareness of ideas and civilizations.   1   2   3   4

i.   improved my ability to think analytically.   1   2   3   4

j.   increased my abilities in oral and written communication.   1   2   3   4

k.   made me feel a part of a community of scholars.   1   2   3   4

l.   reinforced my respect for scholarship.   1   2   3   4

m.   offered me opportunities for advanced, original and specialized work.   1   2   3   4

n.   provided me with flexibility in meeting my individual needs.   1   2   3   4

Did you complete a senior Honors thesis/project? Yes _____ No ______

If yes, rate it as a learning experience on the following scale:
     outstanding _____   excellent ______   good ______   fair ______   poor _______ .

Did your thesis/project provide you with the kind of learning you expected from it?
     Yes _______   No _______

     If no, explain:

Have you published work drawn wholly or in part from your thesis/project?
     Yes _______   No _______

Did your graduate thesis/dissertation grow out of your Honors thesis/project work?
     Yes _______   No _______

**Has your senior Honors thesis/project been a factor in any other way in what you have
done since graduation?**
     Yes _______   No _______

     If yes, explain:

**Now that you've been away for a while, please list two or three Honors instructors who
stand out in your memory and comment on why you remember them.**

     ____________________ -

     ____________________ -

     ____________________ -

Did you participate in a study abroad program while attending Kent State?
Yes _______ No _______

If yes, which program?

Please indicate how effective your study abroad experience was in developing the competencies listed below. Circle the appropriate number using this scale:
(1) very effective, (2) effective, (3) not effective, (4) not applicable.

a.	ability to be flexible and independent	1	2	3	4
b.	ability to relate to people from other cultures	1	2	3	4
c.	ability to see American culture in a new light	1	2	3	4
d.	ability to view issues with a global perspective	1	2	3	4

Have you participated in any international activities or programs (e.g., hosting a student, travel, business) since graduation?
Yes _______ No _______

If yes, what?

During my freshman year: I lived on campus. _______ I was a commuter student. _______

If you were a resident student, did you live in an Honors residence hall?
Yes _______ No _______

If you lived in an Honors hall, rate it as a living/learning experience on the following scale:
outstanding _____ excellent _______ good_______ fair _______ poor _______ .

Did you participate in any volunteer or community service activities while you were in Honors?
Yes _______ No _______

If yes, what?

Are you actively involved in volunteer activities today? Yes_______ No_______

What was the most positive aspect of your experience in Honors?

What was the least positive aspect of your experience in Honors?

If you could change anything about Honors at Kent State University, what would that be?

Are you a member of the Kent State University Alumni Association?
Yes _______ No _______

Would you like more information about the Honors College Alumni Council?
Yes _______ No _______

Is there anything else you would like us to know about you that is not covered in the above questions?

Please attach a business card if you have one and a list of your publications if appropriate. Thank you for completing and returning this survey by <u>August 1.</u>

Alumni Census

Hi! What's new in your neck of the woods? We love hearing from our alumni. Please return this questionnaire. It's like a letter from home for us. Really.

Name: ____

Name while at UNM (if different from above): _______________________________

Alias you would use if you were a TV detective: _______________________________

Address: ____

____

____

Home telephone: _________________ Work telephone: _________________

E-mail address: _________________ Web page: _________________

Family: Spouse or partner's name: _______________________________

(Is your spouse or partner a UHP alum? ☐ Yes ☐ No

Children's names: _______________________________

____

____

Pet names/species: _______________________________

____

____

Education/Institution	Degree	Year Received	Major Field of Study

Awards, Publications, Affiliations, Et Cetera:

____

____

____

It's All about YOU

Where do you work? ____

For how long now? ____

What's new in your life? (Babies, grandbabies, marriages, un-marriages, scandals, promotions, sports trophies won, etc.)

____

____

____

What weird or memorable thing did you do in the past 12 months?

____

____

Do you have pictures of it?   ☐ Yes   ☐ No

Would you be willing to email us one?   ☐ Yes   ☐ No

It's All about US

What was your favorite UHP course? ____________________________

   Why? ____

What was your least favorite UHP course? ______________________

   Why? ____

Which of the following best describes how you felt about the program while you were in it?

☐ Rocked my world!
☐ Bumped my world
☐ Slightly tilted my world
☐ Barely rippled across my world

Which of the following best describes how you feel about the program today?

- ☐ Still rocks my world!
- ☐ Jogs my world
- ☐ Mildly jostles my world
- ☐ Wait a minute...I was in the Honors program?

Which of the following aspects of the program benefited you during your undergraduate career? Mark all that apply.

- ☐ Seminars
- ☐ Teachers
- ☐ Grading Policy
- ☐ H.S.A.C.
- ☐ Advisement
- ☐ Staff Assistance
- ☐ Lectures
- ☐ Physical Space
- ☐ Community Volunteer Activities
- ☐ Senior Options (Colloquium, Teaching, Thesis)
- ☐ Contact with students of diverse disciplines
- ☐ Activities (Conexiones, Sacred Sites, *Scribendi*, Conference Opportunities)
- ☐ Other: ____

Would you recommend the UHP to your son or daughter? Why or why not?

____

____

____

Have you attended any UHP alumni events?   ☐ Yes   ☐ No

If so, which one(s)? ____

How would you rate these events?

- ☐ Spectacular as a fireworks display
- ☐ Spectacular as a bottle rocket display
- ☐ Spectacular as a firecracker display
- ☐ A dud

What obstacles prevent you from attending our alumni events?

____

____

____

Help Us Out Here!

You remember guest speakers, don't you? Those wonderful individuals who volunteered their time to come in and share their fascinating knowledge of some arcane bit of academe? Well, you don't have to be an academic to help UHP students.

Sure, I'm willing to volunteer! Sign me up for:

- ☐ Mentoring
- ☐ Being a guest lecturer
- ☐ Leading a discussion
- ☐ Teaching a seminar
- ☐ Serving on a search committee for faculty, Carruthers Chair, etc.
- ☐ Serving on selection committees for scholarships, fellowships, etc.
- ☐ Serving on Mock Interview panel (usually once a year to prepare students for scholarship interviews)
- ☐ Donation of books, videos, audio/visual equipment, artwork, etc.
- ☐ Donation to the University Honors Program Alumni Endowment

How would you suggest we improve UHP alumni relations?

____

____

____

____

____

____

____

____

____

**Thanks so much for taking time to respond. We know how busy you are.
Don't be a stranger. Stop by in person to say hello sometime!**

APPENDIX L

SAMPLE SITE VISIT REPORT

This sample site visit report was utilized as a training exercise at the 2004 NCHC Institute to train prospective site visitors. The Institute facilitators provided the summarized information about "College #3" (a real, but unidentified, institution) presented below to give a framework from which Institute participants developed a series of questions they would ask during a site visit. Following this exercise, a condensed version of the actual site visit report was provided. (The Honors Administrator at "College #3" gave permission for use of this information, both at the Institute and in this monograph.)

<u>Type of Institution</u> 4-year Private Institution.

<u>NCHC Member</u> Yes.

<u>Attendance at Most Recent NCHC Conference</u> Director, Students.

<u>Undergraduate Enrollment</u> approximately 2,100.

<u>Honors Program Enrollment</u> approximately 150.

<u>Honors Director</u> 0.5 FTE.

<u>Honors Staff</u> part-time student assistants.

<u>Honors Office Facilities</u> Director's office, reception area, conference room/classroom, student organization offices, computer lab, student lounge, storage room.

<u>Operating Budget</u> $44,700 including released time for Director and $15,000 in external funding (private donor).

<u>Honors Program Web Page</u> Yes.

<u>Honors Committee</u> Yes, Honors Committee (includes one student member).

<u>Student Honors Council</u> Honors Student Organization.

<u>Detailed Honors Policies and Procedures</u> Somewhat detailed.

<u>Honors Scholarships</u> None, but Honors students frequently receive scholarships from the College.

<u>Honors Student Research and Professional Development Funding</u> Honors students who have completed 18 Honors credit hours receive $600 per year for research and/or professional development activities.

<u>Honors Alumni Organization</u> No (program is only six years old).

<u>Development Officer</u> No.

<u>Honors Housing</u> Scholar floors in residence hall (but non-Honors students may live there).

<u>Priority Enrollment for Honors Students</u> No.

<u>Honors Advising</u> Yes, provided by Honors Director.

<u>Recruiting and Acceptance into Honors Program</u> Students may be admitted to the Honors Program by the Director or, in the case of some scholarship recipients, by the Director of Admissions without consultation with the Honors Director.

<u>Honors Program Admission Requirements</u>

<u>Entering Freshmen</u> 1220 SAT, 3.60 high school grade point average, or top 10% of graduating class

<u>Continuing or Transfer Students</u> 3.45 grade point average.

<u>Honors Program Retention Requirements</u> 3.45 grade point average (but students with 3.30 may contract courses and remain in Honors Program until it is mathematically impossible for them to reach the 3.45 level at graduation)

<u>Curricular Requirements</u> 26 Honors credit hours, including first-year seminars, interdisciplinary Honors courses, an optional 1-credit thesis preparation course, senior Honors thesis. Honors contracts may be used to transform regular 3-credit courses into 4-credit Honors courses.

<u>Honors Program Recognition</u> Honors courses designated on transcript, medallion at graduation, transcript entry at graduation.

<u>Other Recognition</u> Students (including those not in the Honors Program) also may pursue "Honors in the Academic Major" completely separate from Honors Program. The Honors Program will accept the "Honors in the Academic Major" thesis for the Honors Program thesis.

<u>Honors Program Self-Study</u> Honors Director provided extensive documentation of history and current operations of the Honors program, including how the program fits into NCHC's "Basic Characteristics," supplemented by the background information below.

<u>Background Data Provided</u> College catalog, mission statements for college and Honors program, position descriptions, budget data, course descriptions and syllabi, policies, reports, NCHC and regional Honors participation, evaluation data, Honors office manual.

<u>On-campus Interviews</u> Arranged as requested by site visitors.

COLLEGE #3
HONORS PROGRAM
EXTERNAL REVIEW REPORT
April 6-7, 200X

[Reviewer #1, Name and Institution]
[Reviewer #2, Name and Institution]

I. Introduction

[Reviewer #1 Name, Position at Home Institution, and NCHC Position] and [Reviewer #2 Name, Position at Home Institution, and NCHC Position] were invited by ____________ to serve as outside reviewers for the Honors Program at College #3.

We have divided our report into five sections: (I) an introduction, (II) a brief description of the process of the program review, (III) a general narrative discussing the strengths of the Honors Program, (IV) specific commentary on the structure and organization of the Honors Program, and (V) an analysis of the Program in terms of the National Collegiate Honors Council's "Basic Characteristics of a Fully Developed Honors Program."

II. Process of the Program Review

We requested the following information from ____________ , Director of the Honors Program, by e-mail and asked that the materials be provided at least a month before our site visit:

1. As part of the self-study/planning document, please include a summary of the history of the Honors Program. In addition, please use the National Collegiate Honors Council's "Basic Characteristics of a Fully Developed Honors Program" to assess how your Honors Program meets or does not meet each of the characteristics and how you envision your college's/program's position with regard to each characteristic in the relatively near future.

2. Materials to be Provided in Advance of the Visit (as part of self-study/planning document or as separate documents)
   a. college catalog
   b. mission statement of the Honors Program
   c. position descriptions for Honors Director and Honors office staff
   d. recruiting materials for the college in general and the Honors Program in particular
   e. Honors Program budget for the past five years, including salary for the Honors Director and an average salary figure for assistant/associate deans/directors across campus
   f. Honors Program policies and procedures documents
   g. Honors Program annual reports for past five years
   h. listing and description of Honors courses offered in past five years (if not included in annual reports)

i. longitudinal data of Honors course offerings and student participation in the Honors Program during the past five years (if not included in annual reports)
j. participation in NCHC and regional Honors council activities (if not included in annual reports)
k. evaluation materials used for Honors classes
l. evaluation materials used for Honors advising
m. information about any scholarships or scholarship programs dedicated to Honors students
n. information about links between Honors and overseas programs
o. guidelines or manuals for thesis or creative projects
p. information about any privileges (early enrollment, etc.) that Honors students receive
q. information on role, if any, of the Honors Program in promotion and tenure decisions
r. structure of and administrative policies concerning the student Honors organization
s. facilities of the Honors Program

3. Conversations while on Campus
   a. President of the College
   b. the chief academic officer of the College (Provost)
   c. the Dean of the College
   d. Directors of undergraduate units involved with Honors Program
   e. Honors Program Director
   f. Honors Program office staff
   h. Open meeting with faculty for Honors courses [limited to these faculty]
   i. Faculty and student Honors committees
   j. Open meeting with Honors students [limited to these students]
   k. Others thought appropriate by those responsible for the review process

We appreciate the way in which ______________________ responded to our request for information well in advance of the site visit. Materials provided were comprehensive and organized. They were an invaluable asset in the review process.

Our schedule for the two-day visit included interviews with Dr.___________, Director of the Honors Program; Mr.___________, Registrar; Dr.___________, Dean of the College; Dr. ___________, Associate Dean of the College; Dr. ___________, Provost; members of the Honors Student Organization Executive Committee; Honors Student Staff; members of the Honors Committee and other members of the faculty experienced with the Honors Program; Dr. ___________, Vice President for Fiscal Affairs and Planning; Dr. ________ , Director of Admissions; Mr. ___________, Associate Director of Admissions; and Ms. ___________, Director of Financial Aid. In addition, one of the reviewers met with Dr. ___________, Chair of the Faculty Senate.

In an effort to avoid inadvertent errors on matters of fact, a confidential working draft of this report was sent to the Honors Director by e-mail before the final version was submitted to College #3. Following receipt of the written report, the Provost contacted us about minor errors of fact that are corrected in this amended report.

With more than 700 institutional members, the National Collegiate Honors Council (NCHC) is the largest national organization concerned with Honors education, but it does not serve as a formal accrediting body for Honors Programs or Honors Colleges. The members of the visiting team are NCHC-recommended Site Visitors, and they bring a range of national Honors experience. This document, however, should not be construed to constitute a report from the National College Honors Council as an organization.

III. General Narrative

At every point during our campus visit, we were told of the importance of the Honors Program to College #3. President ______________ referred to it as a "centerpiece program," and literally everyone else with whom we visited noted that the Honors Program had been instrumental in the recruitment of more and better students. The Director of Admissions indicated that the Honors Program was quite important in recruiting new students, and many of the students with whom we visited cited the Honors Program as one of the reasons they decided to attend the College. One student went so far as to state that he/she would not have considered any college that did not have an Honors Program. The students also indicated that they valued the opportunity to interact with other Honors students and faculty in their Honors courses and that they had found their Honors contract experiences to be beneficial. The faculty with whom we met indicated that they found Honors students to have raised the intellectual climate of College #3 in general and that in particular they had enjoyed teaching these students in Honors courses and working with them on Honors contracts. Such unanimity certainly is evidence that the Honors Program is a very good "fit" for College #3 and that the campus community has been able to adjust to having an Honors Program at the College.

IV.   The Structure and Operation of the Honors Program

In this section of our report, we address structural and operational aspects of the Honors Program at College #3. This Honors Program still is relatively young. It originally was proposed as a part of Strategic Planning in 199X, and ______________ was selected as Honors Program Director in 199X. He/she has shaped the Program's development since its inception. The first Honors students were admitted in Fall, 199X. Currently, the Program's enrollment is approximately 150 students.

A. Overall Administrative Support

The Honors Program has a direct line of responsibility to the Provost, a structure that is fully consistent with NCHC Guidelines (see Part V of this report). The Honors Program is a truly campus-wide feature of College #3 that includes both curricular and co-curricular programmatic components.

B. Honors Program Staffing and Budget

The Director is released at half time in order to assume administrative responsibilities for the Program. This model was established in the original proposal when the number of students was half the number currently enrolled. The Director, in addition to working closely with the Honors Committee for program governance, teaches a thesis-preparation course and a noncredit freshman course, serves as Honors advisor for all students in the Program, and is expected to make a significant contribution in college-wide recruitment efforts. It is not clear to the reviewers whether his/her extremely successful performance will count significantly in the promotion process, but to expect a faculty member to invest himself or herself so thoroughly in the position and then not to count it for promotion would be counterproductive. If half-time release based on half the students was appropriate six years ago, it may well be time to reevaluate the adequacy of this release based on programmatic growth.

The responsibility for day-to-day management of the Honors Office's operations is delegated to seven Honors students, supervised by the Honors Director, who by all accounts are dedicated and resourceful. This innovative strategy has allowed the Honors Director to keep the Honors Office open on a full-time basis with minimal budgetary commitment. Although there is general agreement that students gain leadership experience and effectively manage the Honors Office, this approach is at best a stop-gap measure.

To paraphrase the Hoover Commission, "The Honors Director needs help." While Dr. ______________ has done a remarkable "smoke-and-mirrors" job in staffing the Honors Office with seven talented and dedicated student assistants, this is not a viable long-term solution. Providing a secretarial position for the Honors Program would be an important step forward, and it would mean that the Honors Office would be open during summer months instead of just during the academic year. (We would caution against a part-time, shared secretarial position because of the conflicting demands on the secretary's time, but perhaps a 75% time position would be workable for a person who does not wish to have full-time employment.) Having said this, however, we wish to commend the current student employees who have done an excellent job and who recently have created an extensive Honors Office Standard Operating Procedure manual for their successors.

Interest has been expressed in housing additional responsibilities such as prestige scholarship preparation (Marshall, Rhodes, Truman, etc.) in the Honors Program. If College #3 wishes to become competitive for prestigious national and international scholarships, the Honors Program is the logical place in which to center its efforts. Such additional college-wide commitments definitely require reconsideration of the faculty FTE provided for the Honors Program Office. The addition of this function-in and of itself-would justify moving the current Honors Director's position to 75% time, but the 75% release also could be divided between the Director (50%) and an Assistant Director (25%) who would be primarily responsible for the College's scholarship preparation efforts along with other Honors Program duties that might be appropriate assignments. Practice at NCHC institutions varies in this regard. In addition to continuing its NCHC membership, we recommend that College #3 consider joining the National Association of Fellowships Advisors (NAFA) if it wishes to become actively involved in preparing its students for such prestigious scholarships. The NAFA web page link is <http://www.nafadvisors.org/>.

C. Term of Honors Director

Early in our campus visit, we had the impression that the position of Honors Director was intended to be a rotational one with an initial three-year appointment and the possibility of one—and only one—reappointment. As our visit continued, however, we learned from senior administrators and faculty that the director's appointment, like that of department chairs, is a three-year appointment subject to renewal. We know of no Honors Program that is well recognized in NCHC as a leader in Honors education that employs a forced rotation model, and we were relieved to learn that such need not be the case at College #3.

We are aware that some may be concerned that faculty assignments such as that of Honors Director can become "administrative sinecures," but one need only examine the workload undertaken by the current Honors Director (advising, teaching, and program administration) to dispel any such notions with regard to this particular position.

To term-limit an Honors Director who, by apparent unanimous agreement, has done and continues to do a splendid job in his/her position makes little if any sense. To do so for no reason other than "consistency" would be a pronounced disservice to the Honors Program in particular and to College #3 in general.

D. Honors Director Reporting Line

With the restructuring of the central administration at College #3 and the creation of the new Dean of the College position, there has been discussion of having the Honors Director report to the Dean of the College instead of reporting directly to the Provost as is now the case. We believe that this change in reporting line could be problematic at best. The proposed reporting structure would put any Honors Director in a difficult position, having to argue in favor of college-wide priorities when his or her own department chair (sitting in the same administrative committee and also reporting to the Dean of the College) could well take such arguments as being hostile to the more parochial interests of the department.

As we understand the new arrangements, a number of administrators with campus-wide assignments will report to the Provost or President. These would include, by way of example, those responsible for Admissions, Information Technology Services, and the library. We believe that the Honors Director (with his college-wide responsibilities and need to interact with Admissions, Residential Life, etc., on an ongoing basis) occupies a position more analogous to these positions than to a department chair reporting to the Dean of the College.

President _____________ indicated that he/she is considering an approach to seek additional Honors Program funding from a donor who already is providing funds. It therefore would not seem to be an opportune time to "downgrade" the Honors Director in terms of his/her reporting line and thus perhaps send the message that the Honors Program is no longer as central to the College's strategic plan as had been indicated in the past.

E. Possibility of Promotion for Honors Director

The Honors Director is a tenured member of the faculty at the rank of Associate Professor. For the future development of the Honors Program, it is important that success in the role of Director be taken into account in the College's promotion process. We recommend that clear requirements for promotion be developed that take into account the contributions made to the College by successful direction of the Honors Program as part of the overall promotion criteria, remembering that an Honors Director may or may not have his or her department chair as a "champion" in the promotion process (depending upon whether the chair is supportive of the Honors Director's administrative assignment and responsibilities).

F. Admission to the Honors Program

There are clear criteria for admission to the Honors Program, although in practice we under-stand there is greater flexibility than might be understood from merely reading the printed criteria. A point of concern among some faculty was that the Admissions Office has taken on the authority to grant "automatic admission" to the Honors Program for certain scholarship students as part of its recruiting efforts. While we understand and support the Admissions Office's efforts to use the Honors Program as an integral part of its recruiting efforts, we share the faculty's concern about the process for admission to the Honors Program. Admissions personnel stated to the reviewers that they believe that they can identify students who will be successful in the Honors Program through a 45-minute interview, but they did not have any supporting data available during the interview. Neither of the review team members would claim to have such ability, even after long experience in Honors education. Admissions personnel, in response to follow-up questions, indicated a preference for Honors Program admissions including more non-majority students, a better gender balance (recruiting more men), and moving toward more of a "quality mix" instead of so much reliance on standardized test scores. While these criteria may be appropriate for College #3, we believe that the faculty–not the Admissions Office–should be establishing the criteria and making the decisions on admission to the Honors Program. Coordinating Honors Program admissions and scholarships so that the incentives are maximized in recruitment value certainly makes sense, but if a student being considered for a Presidential Scholarship understands that this scholarship confers automatic admission to the Honors Program, it devalues admission to the Honors Program. Furthermore, the Honors Committee and faculty, who can be very helpful in recruitment, are cut out of the process. We recommend that College #3 carefully reconsider the decision that allowed the Admissions Office to grant automatic admission to the Honors Program to recipients of certain scholarships without separate faculty approval from the Honors Program.

We also recommend (as noted elsewhere in this report) that the Honors Director continue to report directly to the Provost. With the Director of Admissions reporting directly to the President of the College, we believe the Director's reporting to the Provost to be particularly important.

It also is worth noting in the context of Honors Program admission and participation that having more female than male Honors students is not unusual. Honors directors are well aware of this pattern, and from time to time questions and responses on NCHC's electronic bulletin board point out that this pattern is more likely the norm than the exception in coeducational institutions. At College #3, with significantly more female than male students enrolled, the pattern is even less surprising.

College #3 can take pride in the fact that it provides an education to many first-generation students. Sometimes, however, these students may not have the stellar records in high school that would qualify them for immediate admission to the Honors Program–but they may perform quite well once they arrive on campus. We recommend consideration of more active recruiting of students who demonstrate their potential by their academic performance in their first and second semesters. A sliding scale could help with the retention figures by providing continuing students with a slightly lower expectation for performance, perhaps a 3.25 grade point average during the freshman year.

G. Facilities

The space allocated to the Honors Office represents a significant improvement over the previous physical location (a single office with a small reception area). In addition to the Honors Director's office, there is a seminar room, offices for student organizations, a study room, a lounge, and storage space. The current Honors facilities are well located in close proximity to the library and academic buildings, and external signage identifies The Honors Program to the public. More elaborate signage would showcase the Program and provide image enhancement as one of College #3's centerpiece programs.

The office space for the Director is reasonably adequate. The space that serves as a class-room and a conference room potentially creates schedule conflicts; however, the space is comfortable for Honors Committee meetings. The computer lab/study area needs to be expanded soon by several more work stations to accommodate the increased numbers of students, and computer upgrades are recommended. The atmosphere in these areas was lively because of the students constantly buzzing around, resulting in a sense of community. The lounge space is attractive, and many students report using this site. One improvement that could be achieved at minimal cost is a new coat of paint to enhance the overall appearance of the Honors Office.

In the longer term, as new buildings are constructed on campus during the next two to four years, moving the Honors Office to space in a more prominent location on campus may well enhance the all-important first impression made on prospective Honors Program students and their families as they consider College #3.

The addition of a seminar room that could also function as a gathering place and meeting room for the Honors Committee would be helpful. We recommend undertaking a long-range plan for a move that would provide more and centralized space to accommodate larger student enrollment (particularly adequate space for the computer workstations and for advising) and the increases in staff position commitment recommended above. Newer above-ground facilities that are close to the library will have symbolic value, make use of attractive traditional architecture consistent with the college, and provide an interior spaciousness that befits the Honors Program. Such facilities will make a clear statement about the importance of academic excellence to College #3.

H. Honors Residence Hall Floor

By providing Honors students with the option to live on a Scholars Honors Floor in the residence hall, College #3 is meeting the needs of approximately 20 academically talented students who seek a residential component to their Honors experience. It is worth noting that many institutions with Honors housing have found over time that demand increases, so we would recommend that advance planning take this possibility into account.

I. Honors Committee

The members of the Honors Committee with whom we met were uniformly positive about the development of the Honors Program during the past six years, and they gave high praise to the leadership efforts of the Honors Director.

The Honors Committee has been, and continues to be, very active in the operations of the Honors Program. The active engagement of these faculty members is a significant programmatic strength. Its membership involves faculty, some of whom are ex officio from other campus committees. The membership of the Provost on the Honors Committee is somewhat unusual in that such committees usually are in the position of making recommendations to the central administration; yet under this arrangement, the Provost would be in effect reviewing his/her or her own recommendations. Another concern of the reviewers is that only a single student has membership on the Honors Committee. We recommend that consideration be given to increasing the number of students on the committee to three or four as a way to achieve balanced representation from the Honors student body.

The Honors Committee has taken on the task of conducting interviews of Honors students at the end of the fall semester, and summarized results were made available to the reviewers. These results were quite typical of what one might expect to find in any Honors Program or Honors college across the country. Honors students usually like their Honors courses, even when they are more challenging than "regular" courses. Honors students also seem likely to be involved heavily in extracurricular activities and leadership positions on campus. Time-management issues are quite common, regardless of institution type or size, as students must adjust to increasing academic demands.

J. Curriculum

At the heart of all Honors curricular experiences is the dedication and creativity of the faculty who teach Honors classes. College #3 has recruited a dedicated Honors faculty who are committed to the notion of Honors education. These faculty are central to the Honors Program's teaching and learning and bear the primary responsibility for promoting, facilitating, and evaluating student learning. Honors teaching presents faculty with opportunities for unique blends in research and teaching and can serve as a curricular laboratory for the College. While the variations among Honors Programs and institutions certainly are wide, characteristically the faculty are interdisciplinary in their approach in many classes.

Based on our interviews and review of syllabi, quality of instruction seems excellent. Faculty are strongly committed to Honors pedagogy through designing interesting courses, engaging students in active learning, challenging students to think freshly and critically, and honing their basic skills. Faculty are appropriately prepared and qualified for the positions that they hold. Most of the faculty hold terminal degrees and evidence ongoing scholarly agendas, e.g., presentations and publications at least within the past six years.

Faculty vitae do not consistently present evidence of Honors scholarship that is typical for young Honors Programs. Ultimately, faculty could be provided with workshops for teaching portfolios. Experts could be brought to campus to create a teaching portfolio for an Honors class. The value of such workshops is increased development of teaching philosophy and Honors methodology. Another forum for faculty development is through the National Collegiate Honors Council publications and annual conference. One faculty member reported that it was attendance at an NCHC conference that convinced him to teach an Honors course. Monographs such as *Teaching and Learning in Honors* are resources that promote curricular development, not only in Honors but also within the broader college community. Data were not evident within this program review regarding the general "non-Honors" faculty's knowledge of the Honors Program and its related mission. This question suggests a need for campus-wide evaluation, possibly in the form of a survey. Faculty may not be fully cognizant of how rich an educational experience is available on their campus.

The Honors College requires 26 Honors credit hours and a 3.45 grade point average for "Honors graduation." Interestingly, however, there is no requirement that students earn any minimum particular grade in their Honors work (Honors courses or Honors contracts) or have a minimum grade point average in that work. It is at least conceivable that a student could meet the current criteria with more "C" grades in Honors work than grades of "A" or "B." Some Honors Programs and Honors Colleges require a minimum "B" grade for Honors work to count toward "Honors graduation," while others require a minimum grade point average in Honors work undertaken. We recommend that College #3 review this aspect of the Honors Program's requirements to determine whether a minimum standard should be established for grades earned in Honors work.

The requirement for a 3.45 grade point average for Honors Program students is a reasonable one, coming near the higher end of the spectrum among NCHC institutions. This is particularly true when, as we understand the process, students (particularly new freshmen) are given some leeway if they fall short of 3.45. An alternative that might be considered is a sliding-scale grade point average requirement that allows a slightly lower grade point average early in a student's career and then moves upward to the 3.45 level for graduation. The advantages of the sliding scale are that it may be somewhat less discouraging to new students and that it would make the entire process somewhat more transparent.

The use of Honors contracts (which allow students by extensive faculty-supervised additional work to transform three-credit courses into four-credit Honors courses) appears to have worked well. Both students and faculty report satisfaction with this approach. College #3s' shift from three-credit to four-credit courses, however, will require reconsideration of this approach. As the Honors Program matures, we recommend that it make every effort to offer more actual Honors courses and decrease reliance on the Honors contract approach.

K. Priority Enrollment

An important feature of many Honors Programs across the United States is priority enrollment for Honors students. This programmatic feature promotes comprehensive curricular development by Honors students, many of whom pursue multiple majors and minors, study abroad, and internship experiences. Without priority enrollment, scheduling difficulties can limit student opportunities and frustrate their laudable goals. We were surprised to learn that College #3 already has de facto priority enrollment through the Professor Permit Process (PPP) mechanism that the Registrar reports involves 4,000 individual computer entries per semester after the paper forms are received in the Registrar's Office. Honors students reported that they make frequent use of the PPP mechanism, particularly earlier in their academic careers. To us, this appears to be a labor-intensive process in the extreme that could rather easily be resolved by allowing Honors students to earn the priority enrollment privilege on a semester-by-semester basis. At a bare minimum, the Honors Director should be able to give electronic clearance to Honors students to enroll in Honors courses without the necessity for a paper form.

Across the nation, even large universities offering a wide range of Honors courses realize that Honors students will have serious class schedule difficulties if they cannot enroll early in the process and build their "regular" class schedule around the Honors courses they are required to take. One of the reasons for the attrition rate in College #3's Honors Program is the frustration students face in fitting everything into their already-crowded schedules—a problem that is likely to increase as a result of the change to four-credit core requirement courses. Add to this the fact that Honors students are among those most likely to engage in double majors, multiple minors, study abroad, and internship experiences and one begins to understand why priority enrollment has come to be seen as a necessity and not a "special privilege" for Honors students. We might add that those institutions providing priority enrollment for their Honors students are not shy about using it as a recruiting advantage.

L. Student Research and Honors Student Development Funds

An Honors student development fund was established for Honors students who successfully complete 15 Honors credit hours. Generally, students reported this was the most important benefit of Honors Program membership. Students described the following uses of this funding: graduate school application fees, parking fees in [City] related to research, laptop computers, membership fees for professional associations, and computer supplies. We recommend the Honors Program consider modifying the use of these funds so that they will more directly support senior theses or capstone experiences. For example, students could submit small grant proposals that document how this funding will be used in their thesis research. The format of such grant proposals would provide experience in writing funding requests and support qualitative development of the project outcomes.

M. Honors Program Web Page

Many prospective Honors students make extensive use of the Internet to gain information as they consider possible colleges and universities, as do students who already have arrived on campus. The web page for the Honors Program <http://www._________> is attractive and informative, but we noted that some of the content has not been updated recently. In addition to the need for updating of some elements of the web page, a suggestion we offer is that the URL be provided to the National Collegiate Honors Council so that NCHC can establish a link from its membership page to the Honors Program web site at College #3. We also recommend that those responsible for the College #3 Admissions web page <http://www._________> develop a link to direct prospective College #3 students to the Honors Program web page.

N. Two-tier Honors Recognition

Graduates of the Honors Program receive a transcript notation and a handsome medallion. In discussions with the Registrar, we learned that it also would be possible to endorse students' diplomas to designate their graduation from the Honors Program. We recommend that this additional recognition on the diploma be implemented.

Many Honors Programs and Honors Colleges provide some form of recognition for their students part way through their undergraduate career. Terms such as "general education Honors" and "general Honors" come to mind. Such early recognition serves to motivate students and quite properly gives recognition for their Honors academic achievements. We believe that it would be worthwhile for College #3 to consider such recognition. There already is something in the way of informal recognition in that only students who have completed sixteen Honors credit hours are eligible for professional development funding, so making the recognition more formal on students' transcripts might not be a major change.

"Honors in the Academic Major" at College #3 already is in place, and we recommend that similar recognition be made available to Honors Program students who do not pursue Honors in the Discipline.

As noted above, at College #3 students may earn recognition through the Honors Program and also earn Honors in the Academic Major. Because Honors in the Academic Major preceded the establishment of the Honors Program, it remains a separate option (although students may use a single senior thesis for both types of recognition). This arrangement is somewhat confusing to students, and we recommend that ways be considered to integrate Honors in the Academic Major into the Honors Program while at the same time retaining appropriate flexibility for departmental faculty and students in their respective majors.

O. Annual Reports

We very much appreciate the voluminous information provided by Dr. ___________ in response to our request for information in advance of our visit to the campus of College #3. As founding Director of a quite-new Honors Program, he/she was able to pull together the data and materials that we needed to prepare for our site visit, but through time this task will become more and more difficult. We recommend that annual reports for the Honors Program be prepared and that these reports be disseminated widely on campus in coming years. We also recommend that these reports be archived as part of the historical record of the Honors Program.

V. The Honors Program in the Context of the National Collegiate Honors Council's Basic Characteristics of a Fully Developed Honors Program

A brief analysis of the Honors Program at College #3 in terms of National Collegiate Honors Council guidelines is provided below. Although it is the largest national organization concerned with Honors education, with more than 700 institutional members, the National Collegiate Honors Council does not serve as a formal accrediting body for Honors Programs or Honors Colleges.

BASIC CHARACTERISTICS OF A FULLY DEVELOPED HONORS PROGRAM

No one model of an honors program can be superimposed on all types of institutions. However, there are characteristics that are common to successful, fully developed honors programs. Listed below are those characteristics, although not all characteristics are necessary for an honors program to be considered a successful and/or fully developed honors program.

A fully developed honors program should be carefully set up to accommodate the special needs and abilities of the undergraduate students it is designed to serve.

This entails identifying the targeted student population by some clearly articulated set of criteria (e.g., GPA, SAT score, a written essay). A program with open admission needs to spell out expectations for retention in the program and for satisfactory completion of program requirements.

_______________'s assessment is correct: the Honors Program has clearly defined admissions criteria suited to the pool of prospective students for the College although how consistently these criteria are upheld by the Admissions Office is unclear.

The program should have a clear mandate from the institutional administration, ideally in the form of a mission statement, clearly stating the objectives and responsibilities of the program and defining its place in both the administrative and academic structure of the institution. This mandate or mission statement should be such as to assure the permanence and stability of the program by guaranteeing an adequate budget and by avoiding any tendency to force the program to depend on temporary or spasmodic dedication of particular faculty members or administrators. In other words, the program should be fully institutionalized so as to build thereby a genuine tradition of excellence.

The Program has an approved mission statement that accords well with the College mission and an ongoing operating budget. The lack of its own personnel budget and its dependence on faculty contracts/appointments in departments may put staffing at risk, or at least create tensions, in the future if departments are shorthanded and resent the administrative load of the faculty member selected as Honors Director. Effective support by the Provost can prevent such a problem.

The honors director should report to the chief academic officer of the institution.

At present, College #3 meets this criterion with a direct reporting line to the Provost. As noted at some length in Part IV of this report, and for the reasons given there, the reviewing team believes that the Honors Director should continue to report directly to the Provost instead of having the reporting line shifted to the new Dean of the College position-even if in some ways the Dean of the College might be considered a "chief academic officer" for many purposes at College #3. (See IV-D, Honors Director Reporting Line.)

There should be an honors curriculum featuring special courses, seminars, colloquia, and independent study established in harmony with the mission statement and in response to the needs of the program.

The curricular design is admirable. The First-Year Seminar is an outstanding cornerstone sequence by all accounts, and the subsequent special topics are interdisciplinary and unique, giving the Honors students unusual opportunities to develop basic skills and integrative and critical thinking. The leadership seminar will bridge effectively the distance between these lower-division courses and the senior thesis. Some programs that lack this bridge lose many of their students who often fail to complete the program partly because of lost momentum. The only concern is the sustainability of this curriculum as sections must be added to accommodate the growing enrollment.

The program requirements themselves should include a substantial portion of the participants' undergraduate work, usually in the vicinity of 20% to 25% of their total course work and certainly no less than 15%.

Twenty-six Honors credit hours are required for graduation. This total represents 23% of the total number of credits required for graduation. As the Honors curriculum is developed, development of core curriculum and integration with major requirements may contribute to increased offerings. Generally, the Honors curriculum is within the standard range, i.e., 15-25%.

The program should be so formulated that it relates effectively both to all the college work for the degree (e.g., by satisfying general education requirements) and to the area of concentration, departmental specialization, pre-professional or professional training.

The program meets expectations well, partly thanks to the structure of the general education requirements for the College. Students reported that not all Honors courses are accepted as credit for the core and "favor" English and history. Such reports are consistent with "early" development of an Honors curriculum. Future goals may consider wider diversity of topics and general education curricular approval. Music majors and Education majors are reportedly challenged to include Honors in their academic programs. This trend is consistent with problems in academic planning inherent within the discipline, e.g., NCATE requirements. Again, future curricular planning may wish to consider the unique needs of these majors, and as a general matter care must be taken across campus not to disadvantage Honors Program students as the College shifts from three-credit to four-credit courses.

The program should be both visible and highly reputed throughout the institution so that it is perceived as providing standards and models of excellence for students and faculty across the campus.

As we have discussed in the earlier sections of this report, from everything we read by way of preparation and encountered during our site visit, the Honors Program is both visible and highly regarded at all levels of College #3. We share the opinion that remarkable progress has been made in the brief history of the Honors Program.

Faculty participating in the program should be fully identified with the aims of the program. They should be carefully selected on the basis of exceptional teaching skills and the ability to provide intellectual leadership to able students.

By all indications, the Honors Program takes care with the faculty selected to teach Honors classes and works closely with these faculty to make certain that they are aware of the Program's goals and adapt their courses appropriately.

The program should occupy suitable quarters constituting an honors office with such facilities as an honors library, lounge, reading rooms, personal computers and other appropriate decor.

The Honors Office space is well organized and serves a number of functions. While it could use a new coat of paint, it certainly is an improvement over the space available to the

Honors Program in the past. If in the next few years, the Honors Office can, as part of overall campus construction and relocations, be moved to a ground-floor suite, it could well be more attractive to students—both those already on campus and those whom the college wishes to recruit.

The director or other administrative officer charged with administering the program should work in close collaboration with a committee or council of faculty members representing the colleges and/or departments served by the program.

The Director works closely with Honors faculty and the Honors Committee, and the Committee meets regularly. We recommend engaging the energy and thought of this group on an ongoing basis for approving courses, planning the academic recognition, and wrestling with the current challenges of an expanding enrollment.

The program should have in place a committee of Honors students to serve as liaison with the honors faculty committee or council who must keep them fully informed on the program and elicit their cooperation in evaluation and development. This student group should enjoy as much autonomy as possible conducting the business of the committee in representing the needs and concerns of all honors students to the administration, and it should also be included in governance, serving on the advisory/ policy committee as well as constituting the group that governs the student association.

The student representation on the Honors Committee could be enlarged, especially as enrollment increases. The Honors Club, however, seems to have a good infrastructure, and students are considering ways to expand membership and student involvement.

There should be provisions for special academic counseling of honors students by uniquely qualified faculty and/or staff personnel.

Advising seems quite satisfactory, and the collaboration with departmental advisors seems to have been strengthened recently. Advising is mentioned as part of the First-Year Seminar. As noted about other aspects of the Honors Program, challenges in meeting students' Honors advising needs will come with increasing enrollment.

The Honors program, in distinguishing itself from the rest of the institution, serves as a kind of laboratory within which faculty can try things they have always wanted to try but for which they could find no suitable outlet. When such efforts are demonstrated to be successful, they may well become institutionalized, thereby raising the general level of education within the college or university for all students. In this connection, the Honors curriculum should serve as a prototype for things that can work campus-wide in the future.

The Honors curriculum is indeed distinct from the rest of the College's curriculum in its use of interdisciplinary, often team-taught, special-topics courses. It is not clear, however, whether this "laboratory" or "incubator" function has had any impact on the rest of the institution. This might be explained by the early establishment of curricular offerings. Honors can effectively model curricular and pedagogical innovations, but it commonly is difficult to take responsibility for spreading them into the larger institution and achieve results without receptive collaborators. During challenging fiscal times, this effort becomes even more difficult. Team-teaching, smaller class sizes, and active learning methods, for example, may simply be seen as too expensive unless they are made an institutional priority. Interdisciplinary courses may also be seen as unwanted competition for traditional courses in the majors.

Finally, it was noted that non-Honors students are permitted to enroll in Honors classes under some circumstances. This enrollment pattern may contribute to the College's community of teaching and scholarship. As the Honors Program grows, this practice should be reconsidered, however, because it influences student benefits and membership within the Honors community. A primary feature of the Honors Program is classes dedicated to academically qualified students, and special care should be given to ways to be certain Honors classes meet these students' needs.

The fully developed honors program must be open to continuous and critical review and be prepared to change in order to maintain its distinctive position of offering distinguished education to the best students in the institution.

The annual and five-year reviews are good tools, and the Director has begun continuous-improvement habits for the Program. The five-year evaluation report was well done. Additional assessment methods would offer greater variety of perspective and a more robust picture of the program. Most important would be the establishment of a course evaluation process distinctive to Honors, all the more helpful given the absence of a mandated institutional student evaluation of instruction except for pre-tenure faculty. This process could be optional and could invite response from both the instructor and students each semester. The Director could be the sole or primary reader of such evaluations, but he or she could summarize them at the end of each year in the annual report. As the program expands, the evaluation of instruction may be even more necessary in order to monitor curriculum quality. A second area of needed assessment is the senior thesis. Currently no examining committee or oral defense is required. Instituting an oral defense (common in many Honors programs) by a committee of three or four faculty members would provide more perspective on quality, but a strong first step would be to provide guidelines to thesis mentors that clarify quality expectations (while maintaining appropriate flexibility), along with an annual meeting of these mentors and perhaps with students-in-progress as well.

A fully developed program will emphasize the participatory nature of the honors educational process by adopting such measures as offering opportunities for students to participate in regional and national conferences, Honors Semesters, international programs, community service, and other types of experiential education.

The Honors Director, other College #3 administrators, faculty, and students have participated in National Collegiate Honors Council Conferences in 2000 (Washington, DC), 2001 (Chicago), 2002 (Salt Lake City), and 2003 (Chicago). As part of their participation, ______________ has presented in several conference venues. Such early and consistent participation in NCHC's Conferences reflects very well on College #3.

______________ has been invited to serve on a "Developing in Honors" Workshop panel at the 200X NCHC Conference in [City] on the topic of "______________________________." This annual workshop is designed for experienced Honors administrators, faculty, and professional staff. From what we have seen during our review of the Honors Program, there is no doubt that he/she will be a valuable presenter for this workshop panel.

In addition to the extensive NCHC participation noted above, three Honors students were presenters at the 200X _______________________________ Regional Honors Conference in _______________________________.

Fully developed two-year and four-year honors programs will have articulation agreements by which Honors graduates from two-year colleges are accepted into four-year honors programs when they meet previously agreed-upon requirements.

This standard is satisfied although we found no separate articulation agreements specific to Honors. Dr. _____________ reports one student has successfully transferred from ___________ Community College. If the articulation is working and community colleges are made aware of the Honors connection (for transfer), there may be no need for a separate articulation document.

ORDERING NCHC PUBLICATIONS

New institutional members receive one copy of each monograph and the NCHC Handbook free with membership. Others should make check or money order payable to NCHC and send to

NCHC
1100 Neihardt Residence Center
University of Nebraska–Lincoln
540 N. 16th Street
Lincoln, NE 68588-0627

I would like to order the following monograph(s) from NCHC (see descriptions on the back of this page):

Monographs *NOTE: 20% discount for 10+ copies of individual monographs*	Member Cost	Non-Member Cost	No. of Copies Ordered	Total Amount Due
Beginning in Honors *advance orders*	$10.00	$12.50		
A Handbook for Honors Administrators	$10.00	$12.50		
Honors Programs at Smaller Colleges	$10.00	$12.50		
Place as Text: Approaches to Active Learning	$10.00	$12.50		
Teaching and Learning in Honors	$10.00	$12.50		
Honors Composition: Historical Perspectives and Contemporary Practices	$10.00	$12.50		
Innovations in Undergraduate Research and Honors Education: Proceedings of the Second Schreyer National Conference	$10.00	$12.50		
NCHC Handbook	$15.00	$20.00		
Two-Year College Handbook *advance orders*	$10.00	$12.50		

Total Amount Paid $ ________

Name ____

Institution ____

Address ____

City, State, Zip ____

Phone__________________Fax ____________Email ____________

Order by phone with a credit card: 402-472-9150.

NATIONAL COLLEGIATE HONORS COUNCIL MONOGRAPHS

Beginning in Honors: A Handbook by Samuel Schuman and George Mariz (Fourth Edition, Forthcoming 2006).

A Handbook for Honors Administrators by Ada Long (1995, 117pp.) Everything an honors administrator needs to know, including a description of some models of Honors Administration.

Honors Programs at Smaller Colleges by Samuel Schuman (1999, 53pp.) How to implement an honors program, with particular emphasis on colleges with fewer than 3000 students (Second Edition)

Place as Text: Approaches to Active Learning edited by Bernice Braid and Ada Long (2000, 101pp.) Information and practical advice on the experiential pedagogies developed within the NCHC during the past 25 years, using the Honors Semesters and City as Text© as models, along with suggestions for how to adapt these models to a variety of educational contexts.

Teaching and Learning in Honors edited by Cheryl L. Fuiks and Larry Clark (2000, 128 pp.) Presents a variety of perspectives on teaching and learning useful to anyone developing new or renovating established honors curricula.

Honors Composition: Historical Perspectives and Contemporary Practices by Annmarie Guzy (2003, 183 pp.) Parallel historical developments in honors and composition studies; contemporary honors writing projects ranging from admission essays to theses as reported by over 300 NCHC members.

Innovations in Undergraduate Research and Honors Education: Proceedings of the Second Schreyer National Conference (2004, 150 pp).

NCHC Handbook. Included are lists of all NCHC members, NCHC Constitution and Bylaws, committees and committee charges, and other useful information.

Two-Year College Handbook by Theresa James (Forthcoming 2005).